To

Bruce Cumings

With my warmest regards,

Hyong Kim

Communist Politics
in North Korea

Ilpyong J. Kim

The Praeger Special Studies program—
utilizing the most modern and efficient book
production techniques and a selective
worldwide distribution network—makes
available to the academic, government, and
business communities significant, timely
research in U.S. and international economic, social, and political development.

Communist Politics in North Korea

PRAEGER SPECIAL STUDIES IN INTERNATIONAL POLITICS AND GOVERNMENT

Praeger Publishers   New York   Washington   London

Library of Congress Cataloging in Publication Data

Kim, Ilpyong J   1931-
    Communist politics in North Korea.

    (Praeger special studies in international politics
and government)
    Includes bibliographical references and index.
    1. Korea (Democratic People's Republic)—Politics
and government.   I.   Title.
DS935.5.K54   320.9'519'3043   72-92887
ISBN 0-275-09190-2

PRAEGER PUBLISHERS
111 Fourth Avenue, New York, N.Y. 10003, U.S.A.

Published in the United States of America in 1975
by Praeger Publishers, Inc.

Printed in the United States of America

To Hyunyong

PREFACE

In an effort to find value-neutral models and paradigms for a comparative study of communist systems, a new group of scholars made a series of attempts in the late 1960s to integrate communist area studies—especially Soviet and East European—with systematic political science. [1] What emerges out of these efforts, however, is not the discovery of a grand theory or new conceptual models, but a plea for rigorous application to communist studies of existing concepts, theories, and models developed by political and social scientists so that specialization in communist area studies may become acceptable to traditional theorists as a subdiscipline of political science. [2]

For the past several years the effort to develop a new theoretical model for the study of communist systems has been in direct response to the inadequacy of the "totalitarian model" on the one hand and, on the other, the behavioral revolution in the discipline of political science. [3] Enough has been written about the totalitarian model in the past ten years to show its weakness because, as Alfred Meyer has stated, "it has not been able to provide adequate explanations of Soviet politics even under Stalin, much less in the last twenty years, either in the USSR or in Eastern Europe." [4] Therefore, in response partly to the need to break away from the value-ridden scholarship of the cold war era and partly to the growing effort of political scientists to be more "scientific," the Soviet and East European specialists have been turning to "behavioralism" so that they may not be alienated from the mainstream of theoretical change in political science. Despite their serious concern with the problem of becoming more systematic and more "scientific" in the analysis of communist systems since the conclusion of the "Symposium on Comparative Politics and Communist Systems" in 1966, the Soviet and communist area specialists are beginning to revert back to their earlier interest in bridging the wide gap between area studies and political science. The unresolved question of how communist area studies can be integrated with the discipline of political science was raised again at the annual meeting of the American Political Science Association in New Orleans in September 1973. A whole panel was devoted to a discussion of "Political Science and Area Studies," including Alfred Meyer's paper on "Comparative Politics and Its Discontent: The Study of the USSR and Eastern Europe" and Chalmers Johnson's "Political Science and East Asian Area Studies." [5]

Meyer, who had urged the Soviet and East European specialists at the 1966 symposium to integrate the study of the Soviet Union and communism with the study of comparative politics, seemed to argue in 1973 that the discipline has not offered the communist area specialists many useful theoretical aids because of a "grave malaise in the contemporary study of politics."[6] The concepts, theories, and models developed by the political scientists have not really met the requirements and expectations of the communist area specialists attempting to apply them to the study of communist political systems. Moreover, Johnson articulated this problem when he noted that what we do have is "style analysis" in the form of "participation rates" in various democracies, majoritarian and consensual processes of political decision making, comparative communist studies, instances of and typical procedures for military intervention in the politics of new nations, "theories" (styles) of representation, reformist and revolutionary modes of mobilization, and so forth. "These tools and correlations are very valuable, but they are not theory," he asserted, "yet it is this 'theory,' actually style analysis, that the area specialist is expected to apply if he wants to gain professional recognition for his work."[7] The failure of political science to build an empirically relevant theory that might be applicable to comparative analysis of communist systems seems to have brought up a new challenge of theory building in the study of comparative politics in the post behavioral era.[8]

Despite the unresolved question of building theory, which is empirically relevant to the study of comparative politics, the Planning Committee for Comparative Communist Studies of the American Council of Learned Societies (ACLS) has made a significant contribution through its quarterly publication Newsletter on Comparative Studies of Communism by stimulating and challenging the communist area specialists to be more concerned with new concepts, approaches, and methods in their analysis of communist systems. Perhaps the most significant thing the ACLS Committee has done to stimulate the student of comparative communist systems is the publication of Change in Communist Systems, edited by Chalmers Johnson.[9] While the new ideas, concepts, and approaches in the study of comparative communism were debated and challenged by the communist area specialists in the early 1970s, I undertook a case study of the communist system in North Korea. Therefore, this book has been influenced by the new concepts and is a direct response to the questions, why is change occurring in the communist system of North Korea, and how has the North Korean leadership managed and administered politically forced development?

The purpose of this study is to analyze the developmental processes by which the North Korean leadership attempted to transform a traditional and backward society into a modern socialist industrial society . Systemic political change seems to have taken place in North Korea in the 1960s, when the leadership perceived that their political institutions were no longer responsive or suitable to the newly emerging social, economic, or value structure of the society. Therefore, they have begun to change these intitutions and behavioral patterns with the introduction of the six-year economic development plan (1971–76) and the creation of a new political structure formed by overhauling the old constitutional order. These changes were designed to increase

role differentiation and to ensure subsystem autonomy, two important
variables of political structure. The development of political institutions had been lagging the social and economic change taking place
at the time when the developmental programs of the 1961-70 period
were being completed. The Pyongyang leadership has come to recognize that the structural and behavioral patterns that evolved in the
mobilization era (1967-70) have outlived their usefulness and relevance
in the new era of mass participation in the 1970s.

    Changes in the communist system of North Korea have taken place
as the leadership engineered them, and the questions of why these
changes are occurring in North Korea and how the North Korean leadership is coping with such changes are the central themes of this book.
We can hardly rely on single-factor theories or unidirectional development to describe and explain why and how the change takes place
in a communist system. However, a combination of what Robert C.
Tucker calls a "cultural approach"[10] and what John Kautsky calls a
"model of communism as a system of forced modernization"[11] is used
in this study as a framework for analysis of North Korean politics.
An approach like this would make it possible for specialists in communist area studies to compare the North Korean experience of modernization with those of other developing societies under communist rule
and also enable them to understand the role and function of communism
in the process of development.

    I hope this book may be characterized as what Arend Lijphart calls
an "interpretative case study" in that I apply some generalization to
the specific case of North Korea with the aim of throwing some light
on it, but the conclusions and propositions of this work are not intended
to generate any hypothesis.[12] It is not a comparative analysis of North
Korea with other communist nations because this study does not systema-
tically compare North Korea's experiences with those of the Soviet
Union or China, although it pays much attention to the idea of "parallel
development" in North Korea and China. This approach might be more
useful in conceptualizing the developmental processes of a traditional
society under communist rule than working from the perspective of North
Korean efforts to emulate either the Soviet Union or Communist China.

    The first chapter is devoted to a survey of the various stages of
development of the past quarter-century (1948-73) so as to have an
overview of North Korea's socioeconomic progress. The second chapter
focuses on the evolution of the leadership structure of the Korean
Workers Party (KWP) and the government, and then discusses the processes by which the ruling elites attempted to transform the political
culture of North Korea. The function of ideology in the process of
transforming the traditional political culture into a new socialist culture has been to inculcate the new attitudes, beliefs, values, and
skills of the North Korean leadership among the masses of the people.
Chapter 3 is devoted to a discussion of "mass line" as a technique of
the North Korean leadership to bridge the gap between ideology and

reality, while Chapter 4 analyzes the conflicts and disputes among the top-level policy makers with regard to priority and strategy of economic development. By analyzing the issues involved in the leadership crisis of August 1956 and comparing it with the 1966 conflict over power and policy, we may be able to come to understand the policy-making processes in Pyongyang and the factional alignment of the time.

In Chapter 5, I have attempted to discuss the overall strategy of economic development of the 1960s, in connection with such organizational techniques as the Chollima (flying horse) workteam movement, the Chongsan-ni method, and the administration of local-level economy. Chapter 6 is a general survey of North Korea's relations with the Soviet Union and the People's Republic of China (PRC) against the background of escalating Sino-Soviet disputes. My discussion covers the period from 1956, when the Sino-Soviet conflict began, to the early 1970s, during which the North Korean leadership gradually developed the policy of independence and self-reliance. The study concludes with the idea that the leadership of any small nation, such as the two parts of Korea, inevitably must adjust and adapt to the changing environmnet of international relations in order to survive. Therefore, the prospect for Korea's reunification in the 1970s depends largely on the stability and durability of the new balance of power being created in East Asia among the four major powers—China, the Soviet Union, Japan, and the United States—whose interests clash on the Korean peninsula.

NOTES

1. See, for example, Frederic J. Fleron, Jr., ed., Communist Studies and Social Sciences: Essays on Methodology and Empirical Theory (Chicago: Rand McNally, 1969), and Robert E. Kanet, ed., The Behavioral Revolution and Communist Studies (New York: Free Press, 1971).

2. See Frederic J. Fleron, Jr. "Soviet Area Studies and the Social Sciences: Some Methodological Problems in Communist Studies," in ibid., pp. 1-28.

3. Alfred G. Meyer, "Comparative Politics and Its Discontent: The Study of the USSR and Eastern Europe," paper delivered at the 1973 Annual Meeting of the American Political Science Association, New Orleans, La., September 4-8, 1973.

4. Ibid., p. 4.

5. Chalmers Johnson, "Political Science and East Asian Area Studies," World Politics, 26, no. 4 (July 1974): 560-575.

6. Ibid.

7. Ibid., p. 12.

8. See Jorgen Rasmussen, " 'Once You've Made a Revolution, Everything's the Same': Comparative Politics," in George J. Graham

and George W. Carey, eds., The Post-Behavioral Era: Perspectives on Political Science (New York: David McKay, 1972).

9. Chalmers Johnson, ed., Change in Communist Systems (Stanford, Calif.: Stanford University Press, 1970).

10. For the cultural approach to the study of communism, see Robert C. Tucker, "Communism and Political Culture," Newsletter of Comparative Studies of Communism 4, no. 3 (May 1971); "Culture, Political Culture, and Communist Society," Political Science Quarterly 88, no. 2 (June 1973): 173-190; and "Communist Revolutions and National Cultures," paper delivered at the RIKA Conference on Comparative Communist Systems: North Korea and East Germany, May 3, 1974, in Ilpyong J. Kim and Henry Krisch, eds., Comparative Communist Systems: North Korea and East Germany (Silver Spring, Md.: Research Institute on Korean Affairs, 1975).

11. See John H. Kautsky, "Communism and the Comparative Study of Development," Slavic Review 25, no. 1 (March 1967): 13-17, and Communism and the Politics of Development (New York: John Wiley & Sons, 1968).

12. Arend Lijphart, "Comparative Politics and the Comparative Method," American Political Science Review 65, no. 3 (September 1971): 688-689.

ACKNOWLEDGMENTS

This study owes a great deal to institutions and individuals, because without their support and sympathy I would not have been able to complete it. I am indebted to the Russian Institute and the East Asian Institute of Columbia University in New York, which generously awarded me fellowships and grants-in-aid that enabled me to study Russian and Chinese language and politics and helped me learn and understand the ways in which Marxism and communism function in different cultural settings when Western ideology and institutions are transplanted to non-Western societies like North Korea and China. My interest in the study of communism in China and North Korea began in the early 1960s, when the ideological conflicts between the Soviet Union and China erupted openly and the North Korean leadership began to assert their policy of independence and self-reliance.

In the course of completing my graduate work at Columbia University, I have written several articles dealing with the communist politics of North Korea for such professional journals as The China Quarterly and Pacific Affairs. However, my serious effort to write a book on the subject of communist politics in North Korea began in the fall of 1970, when the University of Connecticut Research Foundation provided me with a faculty research grant. Dr. Hugh Clark, associate dean of the Graduate School in charge of the Research Foundation, assisted me in the acquisition of documents, source materials, and the Korean, Japanese, and Chinese language magazines and journals used and cited in this study. Had it not been for his generous help in acquiring the source materials, this study would not have been possible.

I am also indebted to Professor Jun-yop Kim, director of the Asian Research Center at Korea University, who encouraged me to continue this work by providing me with materials on North Korea and China. Dr. Young Hoon Kang, editor of The Journal of Korean Affairs and

director of the Research Institute on Korean Affairs, suggested that
I contribute part of this study to his journal, encouragement that
resulted in the publication of two short articles. Revised versions of
these articles have been incorporated in this book. Dr. Augustine
Ch'oe, director of the Institute for Korean Studies in Tokyo, helped
me in obtaining the Japanese materials dealing with North Korea,
while In Duk Kang, director of the Institute for Far Eastern Affairs in
Seoul, rendered his assistance in acquiring the Korean source materials. Bernard Krisher, bureau chief of Newsweek in Tokyo, was kind
enough to let me use his personal file of news clippings and source
materials on North Korea. I am very grateful to them all; however,
they should not be held responsible for any factual mistake or misrep-
resentation I might have committed in this book, for which I am solely
responsible.

Dr. David E. Albright, associate editor of Problems of Communism,
not only encouraged me to carry on my study but also invited me to contribute an article dealing with economic development in North Korea in
1972, a revised version of which is incorporated in Chapter 5 of this
book. I am also grateful to my colleagues in the political science
department of the University of Connecticut, as well as in other institutions, who read certain parts of this book and commented on them at
various stages of my writing.

An earlier version of this study was presented at the Columbia
University Seminar on Modern Korea on February 18, 1972. I would like
to express my appreciation to the participants, who offered constructive
criticism and valuable suggestions.

Finally, my wife Hyunyong and children Irene and Katherene have
been most forbearing and are a great inspiration for my sustained work.
As a token of my appreciation for her patience and encouragement, I
dedicate this modest book to Hyunyong with affection.

CONTENTS

Communist Politics
in North Korea

To commemorate the 25th anniversary of the founding of the Democratic People's Republic of Korea (DPRK), the North Korean leader Kim Il-sung asserted on September 9, 1973, that "for the past twenty-five years (1948-73) our country has been fundamentally transformed. The society has been restructured, the people have been reformed and the natural environment has been changed."[1] Thus he lauded a quarter-century of social, economic, cultural, and political change in North Korea, dividing the historical period into several distinct stages of development: people's democratic reform (1945-48), socialist reform (1953-56), socialist revolution (1957-60), and socialist construction (1961-70). During the socialist construction stage the triple revolution of technology, culture, and ideology was enunciated, a revolution that is moving toward a higher stage of socialist organization in the 1970s.

In order briefly to survey North Korea's political and economic development for the past quarter-century, this chapter will summarize the developmental processes in terms of three main stages. The initial stage involved both the creation of such new political structures as the "people's democratic institutions" (including the party and the government), which replaced the traditional institutions, and the transformation of social and economic structures in the name of the people's democratic revolution. The first stage includes the period from the liberation in August 1945 to the post-Korean War rehabilitation and construction (1953-56), omitting the political events of the Korean War (1950-53). For a scholarly discussion and analysis of this period, one may consult, in addition to the Documents of the Third Congress of the Korean Workers Party (KWP) in April 1956, The Collection of Essays to Commemorate the Fortieth Anniversary of the Great October Socialist Revolution, nine essays contributed by scholars at the Academy of Sciences of the DPRK and published by the Academy of Sciences Publishing House in October 1957.[2]

The second stage of development encompasses the period of the late 1950s and 1960s, during which the socialist revolution was reportedly taking place, the first five-year economic development plan (1957-61) and the seven-year economic plan (1961-67) were being implemented, and socialist industrialization was being carried out—within the span of only fourteen years—an accomplishment comparable to what western societies had taken several centuries to achieve. Full documentation of this period, as well as the documents of the Fourth Congress (September 1961) and the Fifth Congress (November 1970) of the KWP, may be found in The Economic Policy of the Korean Workers Party for the Construction of the Foundation of Socialism in Korea,[3] a collection of essays contributed by the scholars at the Academy of Sciences' Law and Economics Institute, and in The Victory of Marxism-Leninism in Our Country, a collection of articles contributed by North Korean theorists to commemorate the Fourth Party Congress in 1961.[4]

The third stage of development covers the period of the six-year economic plan (1971-76), during which the complete victory of socialism and the construction of communism are projected by the North Korean leadership. In surveying these developments our discussion will focus on the process of institution building and the structural changes in politics and society. The emergence of new political structures and the efforts made by the North Korean leadership to create a new political culture based on the concept of chuch'e (self-identity) constitute the people's democratic system in North Korea.

The goals of reordering social structure and of building a new organization, whose primary function was to bridge the gap between the ideology of the new leadership and social reality, were the priorities of the North Korean leadership when they came to power in 1945 under the protection of the Soviet occupation forces. In his own analysis of Korea's social structure, Kim Il-sung perceived that Korea is basically a backward and agrarian society in which the capitalist form of economy had not been able to develop, partly because of the feudal or semifeudal character of the economic system and partly because of the exploitative colonial rule of the Japanese government. Therefore, in order to build a new society, Kim concluded, the traditional economic and social structures should be completely overhauled and new institutions created. By abolishing feudal land-ownership in the countryside, the North Korean leadership began to emancipate the peasantry from exploitation by the landlords. Hence, the peasants had to be liberated and the land expropriated, since the peasants were too poor and passive to join the efforts of the new leadership to change the economic and social structure, and the land-owners were unwilling to invest in industrial development. Traditional life styles and old beliefs had to be altered by instituting a series of reform programs to accompany the work of institution building.

THEORY OF THE PEOPLE'S DEMOCRATIC SYSTEM

In search of significant and original contributions made by Kim Il-sung to the general theory of Marxism-Leninism, North Korean scholars and theorists came up with the idea that North Korea's unique national liberation movement and people's democratic revolution under his leadership should be considered Kim's major contribution to the theory of Marxism-Leninism.[5] The literature dealing with Kim's original contribution to the theory of Marxism-Leninism suddenly proliferated in 1972; in addition, five volumes of the collected works of Kim Il-sung were published in Japan to celebrate his 60th birthday in April 1972. What emerges from these writings is that Kim Il-sung is "a great leader" and "an unprecedented genius," because in his development of the theory of revolution he was able to apply creatively the universal theory of Marxism-Leninism to the unique and specific conditions of North Korea. Thus, Kim's theory of revolution is an original and new theory that is based on his ideology of chuch'e (self-identity), encompassing the concepts of independence in politics, self-reliance in economy, and self-defense in military affairs.

The dual concept of revolution—national liberation on the one hand and, on the other, the people's democratic revolution—was said to have originated from Kim's unique experience of coping with specific Korean problems. Since Korea has been under foreign domination, first by the Japanese military and then by the American "imperialist" occupation, for the past sixty years, Kim's theory of national liberation grew out of the anti-Japanese struggle between 1931 and 1945, while the theory of people's democratic revolution derived from the experience of building the people's democratic system to drive out the American occupation forces from 1945 to 1972.[6] Therefore, the theory of people's democratic revolution has been developed in the process of applying creatively the general principles of Marxism-Leninism to the unique and concrete situation of liberated Korea. What, then, is the underlying concept of people's democracy that shaped and influenced the development of the political system in North Korea for the past quarter-century?

Following liberation after 35 years of Japanese rule, Korea achieved neither the independence nor the self-governmnet for which Koreans had fought for more than three decades, but was occupied by the two allied powers. The Soviet Union occupied the northern half of the Korean peninsula, while the United States controlled the southern half; the dividing line was the 38th parallel. The Soviet occupation forces under Commanding General T. Shtykov provided the most favorable conditions, as Kim Il-sung himself acknowledged, for the creation of new political institutions[7] by the new communist leaders.

In North Korea, unlike Communist China, Yugoslavia, and North Vietnam, the mode of coming to power was determined by an outside force rather than growing from inside through a long and arduous struggle to win and mobilize the support of the masses and organize them to carry out revolutionary change. Since the North Korean leadership was imposed from outside, it required the legitimization of its own rule so that it could win the support of the people. The people in North Korea believed that political power actually grew out of the barrels of Soviet guns after the Japanese surrender. The people's democratic system was, therefore, a direct effort to resolve the problems of legitimization: winning and organizing the support of the people in North Korea. The ultimate goal of the new leadership, thus, was to build a new political system in which "all the workers, peasants, soldiers, and working intellectuals would become the actual holders of state power in the country, and exercise that power to defend their independence and take direct part in state administration and politics"; this has become a reality after a quarter-century of hard work. [8] Thus President Kim Il-sung was proud to assert, after twenty-five years of personal rule, that "the Democratic People's Republic of Korea is governed by the people themselves and is truly the first state of the whole people in the history of Korea because it serves the entire people." [9]

The underlying concept of people's democracy also involved the notion of a transition from semifeudal and colonial society to the socialist system without passing through the stage of capitalist development. The capitalist system had never been developed because of the Japanese occupation of Korea, and therefore Korea was not ready for a bourgeois democratic revolution. Even though some Marxist theorists, who were later denounced as right-wing opportunists, advocated the development of capitalism before the establishment of the socialist system, the North Korean leadership devised the stage of people's democracy in order to avoid a capitalist transition period between feudal and colonial society and socialism.

In North Korea in 1945, the peasantry constituted more than 80 percent of the total population, while the industrial workers accounted for only a small fraction of the working class. Therefore, an alliance between the industrial proletariat and the peasants was necessary in order to build the broadest possible base of mass support. The united front policy was, thus, closely linked with the concept of people's democracy. In the early phase of the united front, Kim Il-sung told the party representatives of the five provinces in North Korea that "in order to construct the Democratic People's Republic of Korea we must establish a united front consisting not only of the working class and the peasantry but also of all the patriotic and democratic forces including the national bourgeoisie . . . . thus we should be able to win over the masses to our side." [10]

The group of communists led by Kim Il-sung was only a small fraction of the political forces operating in liberated Korea, even though they were supported by the Soviet Union; they therefore adopted a united front policy through which the concept of people's democracy was to be implemented. The twin goals of reordering the social structure and building institutions of people's democracy were attained by means of the democratic revolution and the establishment of people's committees at various levels of government. The united front was, thus, used as the organizational method of building the KWP and the People's Committee (government), as well as the rationale for the execution of such reform programs as land redistribution, nationalization of industry, labor legislation, and the emancipation of women in North Korea.

Because the united front served as the organizational principle of building the party and government, Kim Il-sung devised the idea of "core leadership and membership" in institution building. The core members of the North Korean Communist Party in 1945 consisted of veteran communists, under the leadership of Kim Il-sung, who had carried out the anti-Japanese armed struggles in the 1930s and 1940s.[11] This group later served as the leadership core of the North Korean Party while the other party members were recruited and trained.

The membership of the North Korean Party, therefore, included communists who had participated in underground activities in Korea during Japanese colonial rule, a large number of whom were imprisoned but were released after the liberation of Korea; and those who were exiled abroad but took part in various anti-Japanese movements, such as the communist and independence movement in China and Russia, but now returned home to join the newly created communist organization. Thus, the composition of the Party's membership and leadership was extremely heterogeneous. Of the total membership of about 4,530 in the North Korean Communist Party in 1945, industrial workers accounted for less than a third (30 percent), while the peasants made up 34 percent and the petit bourgeoisie, intelligentsia, businessmen, artisans, and the like accounted for 36 percent. This was an indication of why the North Korean party stepped up its rectification campaigns to purify the party structure.

Because of the heterogeneous tendencies in the party structure, the party leadership encountered a variety of organizational problems. Recurring problems of organization included the opportunistic tendencies of some leaders, apparently encouraged by factionalism; local and regional sectarianism; and family-type operation based on nepotism. There were also problems of communication because the party's policy directives often failed to reach the local units. Communist organizations sprang up in various provinces of Korea in 1945, when the communist leaders were released from Japanese prisons and the exiles returned from abroad to start the movement. The newly organized party became locally quite autonomous in its leadership and organization. Thus, Kim's core group was unable to extend its full control over the so-called domestically bred communist leaders and organization in the embryonic stage of institution building.

Therefore, Kim and his followers immediately began to create a unity and solidarity between the party's core members and the domestically bred communists. In spite of the efforts made by the Central Organization Committee of the North Korean Communist Party, set up on October 10, 1945, under the leadership of Kim Il-sung, to create party unity by means of iron discipline and democratic centralism, organizational problems persisted as a result of the party's heterogeneity. In response to these problems, united front tactics were used to solidify the general membership and establish unity between the core members and other members.

When the first organizational meeting was called on October 10, 1945, with the participation of delegates from five provincial committees, the Central Organization Committee (sometimes called the North Korean Bureau of the Korean Communist Party) was set up with representatives of various factional groups. The four dominant groups of Korean communists were represented by their leaders. The so-called indigenous group (or domestic faction) was represented by Hyon Chun-hyok and Chang Si-u; the group that had returned from the Soviet Union (or the Soviet-Korean faction) was represented by Ho Ka-yi and Nam Il; while the group that had returned from China (or the Yenan faction) was represented by Kim Tu-bong and Ch'oe Ch'ang-ik. Kim Il-sung and his followers (the Kapsan faction) seem to have played the most influential role in the founding of the North Korean Communist Party. At this meeting one of the Soviet-returned group, Kim Yong-bom, was elected to serve as acting secretary of the newly organized party. Kim Il-sung failed to get himself elected party secretary, but at the Third Plenary Session of the Central Organization Committee on December 17, 1945, he succeeded in becoming secretary, and at that time officially named the party the North Korean Communist Party. [12]

In the process of building the party's new structure on the basis of the united front, Kim Il-sung and his associates immediately began to establish unity between his core members and other groups. In February 1946 the North Korean Communist Party merged with the New People's Party (Sinmin Tang), a party of liberals and Yenan returnees headed by Kim Tu-bong (the leader of the Korean Independence League in Yenan, China, and the head of the New People's Party) chairman of the new party. Kim Il-sung and Chu Yong-ha, a leader of the domestic-bred communists, were elected vice chairmen of the newly merged party. The seven-member Politburo of the new party, the ultimate organ of decision making, included the chairman and two vice chairmen of the party, and four other members who represented the dominant factional groups. [13]

After the South Korean Workers Party (formed by the merger of the Communist Party, the People's Party, and the New People's Party in South Korea in 1948) was outlawed by the South Korean government and took refuge in North Korea, it merged with the North Korean Workers Party in 1949, establishing the KWP. After the merger, Kim Il-sung

was formally elected to the chairmanship, and Pak Hon-yong (leader
of the domestic-bred communists and the head of the South Korean
Workers Party) and Ho Ka-yi (leader of the Soviet-returned group)
became the KWP's two vice-chairmen. The important question of why
Kim Il-sung was successful in seizing full control of the KWP may not
be answered fully, but it was due largely to his demonstration of leadership skill and organizational ability in recruiting and building up his
own supporters and followers around the party's core members and
entrenching them not only in the provincial party committees but also
in the local party organizations at the lower level. Furthermore, Kim
was able to build up his loyal supporters in the People's Committee
(the government bureaucracy) at various levels from the village to the
central people's committee. Under the united front policy the membership of the party increased rapidly from 4,530 in 1945 to 750,000 in
1948, and a majority of the new members were able to acquire new
status in society because of Kim's united front policy.

The concept of mass participation as part of the united front policy
was more explicitly reflected in the development of governmental institutions during the democratic reform period. The creation of the Democratic People's Republic on September 9, 1948, itself seemed to imply
that the new government was by no means a dictatorship of the proletariat like that created by Lenin in the Soviet Union, but a government
by united front (or a coalition government) comparable to what Mao
Tse-tung had created on the basis of the idea contained in his "On
New Democracy" (January 1940) and "On Coalition Government"
(April 1945). Many observers of North Korean politics in the 1950s
tended to disregard the influence of Mao Tse-tung's political thought
on North Korea's efforts to build new institutions because of the
Soviet occupation of North Korea. Many students of communist politics accepted the myth that Kim Il-sung was nothing but a puppet of
the Soviet Union and the stooge of the international communist movement. [14] However, one can hardly ignore the impact of Mao's political
thought on the development of North Korean political institutions,
because the nature and characteristics of these two societies, backward and predominantly agrarian, were quite similar; and the problems
of creating new values and institutions to replace old ones have been
shared by both leaders, Mao in China and Kim in North Korea. Thus,
parallel development, not necesarily emulation, was quite apparent
in the late 1940s and 1950s.

The basic principle of government was said to be the realization
of full and free expression of the popular will through the mechanism
of representative organs, from the village-level people's assembly to
the top-level Supreme People's Assembly. The people's assembly,
thus, functioned as a communication channel through which linkage
between the popular will and the central policy was established. Therefore, the structure of the democratic people's government was based
on the principle of mass participation. Thus, the people's democratic

government was a coalition of indigenous nationalists, communists, socialists, and even religious groups. In the new government no single group or faction dominated the political process, and the leadership structure was set up with a coalition of four powerful groups: the Soviet-returned group, the Yenan-returned group, the domestic-bred communists, and the guerrilla group led by Kim Il-sung.

The Soviet policy toward Korea during the democratic reform period was aimed, as in the case of the East European countries, toward the creation of a coalition government including the right and left factions of the nationalists. [15] Even the 32-member People's Political Committee set up in South Pyongan Province in August 1945 had 16 members each from the nationalist and communist groups in North Korea. [16] This committee functioned as the government and administrative agency that was headed by the most prominent leader of the nationalist group (Cho Man-sik), while the communist leaders took up such cabinet posts as internal affairs, the judiciary, and the secret police. This committee took over all of the administrative functions in North Korea during the political vacuum created by the withdrawal of the Japanese rulers.

The Political Committee was gradually expanded to include delegates from the Communist party, other political parties, social organizations, and representatives elected from the people's committee at each level, from the village to the province. This committee was finally converted to the North Korean Provisional People's Committee (PPC) on February 8, 1946. The primary function of this organization, somewhat similar to that of the People's Political Consultative Conference of China, was to lay the groundwork for the establishment of government and administrative systems in North Korea. This committee, characterized as the center of the people's power because it included the broad antiimperialist and antifeudal democratic forces in North Korea, made a declaration of the fundamental policy for the forthcoming constitutional government in the form of a "Ten-Point Program" and became a kind of people's democratic dictatorship. This policy was later incorporated with Kim Il-sung's "Twenty-Point Program" to become the basic policy line of the North Korean government.

Since the Twenty Point Program served as the foundation on which the 1948 constitution of the DPRK was drafted, it should be discussed here in the general context of governmental development in North Korea. The program set forth the economic, cultural, administrative, and foreign policies of the DPRK. It defined "the interests and welfare of the people in every aspect of the political, economic, and cultural spheres" and established the so-called "democratic policy line of the entire Korean people." [17] Under such broad guidelines the character of that stage of the Korean revolution was defined as "an antiimperialist, antifeudal people's democratic revolution." The remnants of Japanese rule were to be thoroughly liquidated, and those who had opposed the Korean independence movement by collaborating with the Japanese colonial government were to be completely eliminated from participation in the political processes of the new regime.

The North Korean leaders in both the communist and nationalist camps seemed to perceive that the Provisional People's Committee, as a genuine coalition of various interest groups, would function as the central government and perform the fundamental tasks of administering the economy and society until the constitutional government was formally established. However, a group of people who had, in the past, collaborated with the Japanese colonial rule, the national traitors, compradore capitalists, and feudalistic landlords were singled out as the antirevolutionary forces of North Korea and were excluded from taking any part in the stage of people's democratic revolution.

Because of the unique characteristics of Korean society and its revolutionary condition, the Provisional People's Committee was said to have been established to ensure that the goal of the revolution was achieved in good faith. To ensure this outcome, the People's Committee became a symbol of the people's democratic power, through which the broadest possible masses would take part in the administration of such mass-oriented political programs as land reform, labor reform, and nationalization of industry. "The People's Committee (government) at each level is the broadest belt which links the Party and the masses, the executor of our Party's line and policy, and the master of the house responsible for the people's livelihood," said Kim Il-sung in defining its function. [18]

The People's Committee in North Korea as a form of popular government was far more democratic and inclusive in its organizational structure and functions than the government that had emerged in the Soviet Union after the Bolshevik Revolution. The Soviets were led exclusively by the proletariat, allied with the peasants and exercising the dictatorship of the proletariat. "The Provisional People's Committee of North Korea is the people's government established by the principle of democratic national united front," Kim Il-sung sserted, "and it encompasses the broad antiimperialist, antifeudalist, and democratic forces on the basis of the worker-peasant alliance led by the working class." [19]

In explaining the underlying principles of the people's democratic system in North Korea, Kim Il-sung offered his own thoughts on the operational procedures of the people's committee. "This committee is a form of government, organized by the people themselves for the purposes of protecting their own interests and of fighting for their own freedom and happiness," Kim stressed. Therefore, "this government maintains a close link with the people, its activities depend exclusively on the support of the people, and its existence depends on the full support of the masses. The people's government performs the function of enabling the broadest possible masses to participate in governmental activities and of bringing them close to the people." [20] Though the structure of government has changed considerably during the past quarter-century, the concepts of popular government and mass participation still serve to define the people's democratic system in North Korea.

— something is missing here — a lot of slogans, but little substance; what's the problem?

SOCIALIST CONSTRUCTION AND STRUCTURAL CHANGE

Socialist reform programs of 1945-48 brought about drastic changes in the economic as well as social structure of North Korea. In the industrial sector, the factories, transportation facilities, communications systems, and financial institutions, which had been owned and operated by the Japanese colonial authorities and/or the compradore capitalists, were immediately nationalized by the newly created people's committee (government) so as to create the so-called people's economy and increase productivity. Between 1946 and 1949, public ownership of industry increased from 72.4 percent in 1946 to 90.7 percent in 1949, while private ownership of industry decreased from 29.6 percent in 1946 to 9.3 percent in 1949. Thus, by the end of the democratic reform period more than 90 percent of the industrial sector of the economy was converted to state ownership.

Structural change in rural society had already begun to occur during the democratic reform period when the land reform program was instituted in March 1946. Before the implementation of the land reform program, about 80 percent of all the arable land was owned by only a small fraction (3.3 percent) of the agrarian population, and 80 percent of the people (approximately 2.4 million peasant families) were either tenant farmers or poor peasants who owned no land. About one million chongbo (hectares) (one hectare equals 2.2 acres) of land owned by the landlords were appropriated by the people's government, and 98.1 percent of this was distributed equally to the tenant farmers, poor peasants, and small landlords in compliance with the land reform legislation. Thus, more than 720,000 peasant families were said to have benefited by the land redistribution. The remaining 1.8 percent (about 18,000 hectares) were turned over to the provincial and county people's committee for public ownership. [21]

In carrying out land distribution the number of family members, as well as the number of working hands in each family, was taken into account, according to official statements, in order to establish the procedure of equal distribution of land and to eliminate certain inequities in the private ownership of farm land. As a result of the land reform program, all vestiges of colonial and feudal land ownership were reportedly wiped out, and a new land ownership system was established in the countryside. [22]

In this stage of democratic reform, the peasant and agrarian questions consisted of emancipating the peasants once and for all so that they could not be exploited and oppressed again, and freeing the working forces of the agricultural sector from the shackles of the old system of property ownership by liquidating capitalist elements in rural society and reorganizing the system of land redistribution with an eye to restructuring the individual type of peasant economy and creating a socialist collective economy at the final stage of socialist revolution.

Following the Korean War (1950-53), which not only brought about the total destruction of the economic and industrial base but also shattered the whole framework of the society, the North Korean leadership embarked on postwar reconstruction and development programs from 1953 to 1956, a period commonly known as the stage of socialist reform. By the end of 1956, with the massive economic and technical assistance provided by the Soviet Union, Communist China, and the East European countries, North Korea was able to restore its economy to the economic level of the prewar year 1949 because the KWP had adopted an economic policy of "maximum production with maximum savings."[23]

The growth of industrial production in the postwar period (1953-56), as well as in the period of socialist revolution (1957-61), has been recorded as the most impressive achievement of the socialist societies. Industrial production showed an average increase of 42.2 percent annually during the first three years (1957-59) of the five-year economic plan) period (1957-61). North Korea therefore claimed that industrial production in 1960 was 7.7 times greater than in 1949. "The reason why we achieved such glorious results in 1957 was not because of policy decisions," Kim Il-sung asserted, "but because of the fact that the Party's Politburo and the Central Committee members, Vice-Premiers, Ministers, and high ranking cadres of the government participated directly in discussions with the working people and listened to their creative opinions and suggestions for the correct implementation of our policy line."[24]

The agricultural cooperative movement as the means of restructuring rural society was launched in 1954 with the twin goals of increasing socialist consciousness among the peasantry, which lagged that of industrial workers, and increasing agricultural productivity. Three types of model cooperatives were initially introduced to encourage the peasants to join the cooperative movement of their own free choice. The first type was a simple mutual aid organization in which land and draft animals were shared for the purpose of easier farming. This type was considered an embryonic phase of the socialist economy. The second type was a semisocialist farm in which the land, farm implements, and draft animals were collectively owned by the cooperatives, but the farm products were distributed on the basis of the amount of property each member contributed to the cooperative. In the third type, land, farm implements, and draft animals were collectively owned by the cooperative and the products of the cooperative distributed to each member on the basis of the amount of labor he or she contributed rather than the amount of properties contributed.[25]

By the end of 1954, approximately 31.8 percent of the peasant households had joined farm cooperatives, more than 78.5 percent of which were in the third category. The movement expanded rapidly, and by the end of 1965 approximately 81 percent of the peasant households had joined cooperatives; of these 97.5 percent were in the third category.[26] According to the official account, as a result of this rapid cooperative movement grain production increased beyond expectations and food problems were almost entirely resolved by the end of 1956.[27] It was also claimed that by August

1958 the entire peasant population had joined agricultural cooperatives and that industry and commerce were totally socialized by the end of that year, a date that marked the completion of socialist reforms and the beginning of the socialist revolution in North Korea. [28] Beginning in September 1958, the industrial workers and the peasants had been transformed into socialist workers, since their wages were based on their work points rather than their contribution of property to the cooperatives. Thus, the economis system is said to have been transformed into a socialist economy by the end of 1958.

Since the rural population of North Korea consisted mainly of poor and middle peasants (poor peasants accounted for 40 percent; the middle peasants, 59 percent) and fewer than 0.6 percent of the peasants were rich, the rich peasants were encouraged to give up their properties to cooperative management and to submit themselves to the reform programs of "education through labor." Unlike the kulaks of the Soviet Union, the rich peasant were neither harrassed to give up their land nor pressured to join the agricultural cooperatives, but they were said to have been persuaded and educated to support the government policy of surrendering their properties. [29] However, according to some landowners who suffered bad experiences and took refuge in South Korea, pressure tactics and terror were used to extract the farmland from the landlords for redistribution, but the rich peasants were educated and persuaded to give up a portion of their land for redistribution. Obviously, there is no way of measuring the extent of resistance on the part of the landlords and the rich peasants in their effort to keep their private property, but the official account creates the impression that the peasants were fully persuaded of the advantages of cooperative farming through a series of experiments in three types of cooperatives. In addition to agricultural cooperatives, the North Korean leadership organized a producers' cooperative for the handicraft industry and consumers' cooperatives for industrial goods in an attempt to win the support of the common people.

By amalgamating the small cooperatives at the village level, which included an average of 79 households, the North Korean leadership created a larger unit at the li (township) level encompassing more than 275 households in each cooperative. Thus, the amount of arable land in each cooperative increased from 133 hectares to 406 hectares by October 1958. The drive for the amalgamation of the cooperatives at the level of the basic administrative unit (li) was thus launched at the same time that the unification of the administrative tasks of the hsiang (the Chinese equivalent of the North Korean li) government and those of the commune in China was accomplished under the Great Leap Forward policy. The parallel development in China and North Korea during the 1957-61 period was quite apparent as the cooperative farm movement, the Chollima (flying horse) movement, and the Chongsan-ni method were carried out.

The revolutionary change in economic and social structure had already begun to shape up by 1958, when the socialization of agriculture and industry was completed, and the seven-year economic development plan (1961-67) was being formulated in 1960. In summing up the great achievements of the 1957-60 period, North Korean scholars asserted that "the great high tide of socialist construction means a radical change at the maximum speed in every sphere of our people's socialist construction encompassing alteration in politics, economics, culture, and ideological consciousness as well as the great upsurge in our people's enthusiasm for government by the whole people."[30] The successful achievement of the five-year economic plan (1957-61), which is claimed to have been accomplished in three years, was thus attributed to two important factors: the unleashing of the people's creative wisdom and energy and the launching of the mass political movement in the form of the Chollima workteam movement. Therefore, the high tide of revolutionary upsurge was actually meant to break as fast as possible away from the traditional way of life and eradicate the remnants of old values, beliefs, and institutions.

In the course of casting away the traditional social structure, eliminating the outmoded ideological consciousness, eradicating the old-fashioned way of life, and also bringing about changes in the old-fashioned techniques, methods, and styles of work-efforts which were essential to progress toward industrialization and modernization—the North Korean leadership launched the triple revolution of technology, culture, and ideology in the late 1950s and elevated it to a mass political movement in the 1960s. Since the material condition of revolutionary change was said to have been provided by the successful completion of the five-year economic plan, new attempts at institution building were designed to cope with the changing environment of the economic and social system. The fundamental goals of the technical and cultural revolution, adopted as the policy line of the KWP at the Plenum of the KWP Central Committee in September 1958, were to eradicate conservatism, passivity, and ignorance about technology, which were perceived as the main obstacles to socialist industrialization.[31] However, the tactical goal of the technical and cultural revolution in 1958 was simply to arouse the revolutionary consciousness of the working class to enhance their incentives for increased productivity in industry and agriculture so that the five-year plan might be completed two years ahead of schedule, a target that was said to have been attained in 1959.

By unleashing the creative wisdom and energy of the working people and arousing the revolutionary enthusiasm of the entire population, the North Korean leadership made a serious attempt to double or triple the workers' capability and efficiency. Such machines as tractors, trucks, excavators, and bulldozers were produced for the first time in Korean history, and this was achieved with exclusive utilization of North

13

Korea's own resources and techniques. Therefore, the North Korean leadership proclaimed proudly that in 14 years North Korea had been able to accomplish a degree of socialist industrialization that had taken centuries in western society.[32] The completion of the five-year plan was said to have elevated North Korea from a backward and agrarian society to an advanced industrial-agricultural state in which the entire people owns the means of production and operates it under the principle of self-reliance and self-sufficiency.

The technical and cultural revolution—unlike the cultural revolution in China in 1966-69—was designed to improve the technical skills and cultural standards of the working people. Why was it necessary to have the technical and cultural revolution as early as 1958? "In a country like ours, which has not passed the stage of capitalist development and is still considered a backward and agrarian state," Kim Il-sung responded, "the people must seize the sovereign right and then carry out the technical revolution after the socialization of all means of production."[33] Thus, in a backward and agrarian society like North Korea in the 1950s, the leadership came to grips with the basic problem of socialist industrialization: Technical revolution is an essential element because it requires the construction of a heavy industrial base, of which the machine-building industry is a key component.

In carrying out the tasks of technical revolution, the North Korean leadership was said to have combined the effort of improving and expanding existing industry with the effort of creating new industrial plants requiring new technology and modern equipment. Priority was given to heavy industry in the modernization and mechanization program. The process was gradual as the piecemeal mechanization of industry brought about total mechanization and automation. In the rural areas, on the other hand, technical revolution included programs of irrigation, electrification, mechanization, and "chemicalization" of agriculture.

The process of carrying out the technical revolution went through two important stages: preparation and full implementation. In the preparatory stage, priority was given to heavy industry and machine building; these served as the technical foundation on which the people's economy was to be built. In the rural sector, the irrigation and electrification programs had priority in the preparatory stage. In the second stage, however, every aspect of industry was encouraged to introduce new techniques and modern equipment. There was continued emphasis on the development of heavy industry and machine building, as well as such infrastructures as the constuction business, transportation facilities, and maritime industries. The technical reforms and assistance programs were, thus, implemented not only in the basic industrial sector but also in all branches of national economy.

However, the machine building industry took the lion's share of the state investment as it continued to serve as the main thrust of the technical revolution. Kim Il-sung said, 'The central consideration of developing all sectors of industry such as electric power, steel, coal mining, chemicals, and agriculture is actually to develop the machine-building industry. Thus the technical revolution means greater expansion of the machine-building industry because the machine determines everything."[34] The output of the machine-building industry, therefore, increased quickly from 17.3 percent of the gross industrial output in 1956 to an impressive 21.3 percent of the gross industrial output in 1960. Between 1961 and 1965, the output of the machine-building industry increased 2.7 times over that of 1960.[35] By the end of the seven-year economic plan, North Korea claimed to have produced such heavy machinery as 6000-ton presses, 10 to 25 ton heavy trucks, 75-horse-power tractors, $4-M^3$ excavators, 5000-ton ships, and electric and diesel engines for railway trains. More than 100 machine-building plants had been newly constructed, thus making it possible to export all kinds of machine products.[36]

Under the slogan of technical revolution, irrigation and electrification programs in rural areas were basically completed by the end of the five-year plan, enabling North Korea to suppy electric power to every township (li) throughout the country. The production of tractors was reported to have increased from 8,050 to 12,500 in 1960 alone, and that of other farm machinery tripled—from 3,000 to 9,000 units—in the same year.[37] Thus, by the end of the seven-year economic plan in 1969 the countryside was supplied with tractors, trucks, modern farm equipment, and weed killer, and the number of tractors per 100 hectares of arable land reached 2-2.5, a number projected to increase to 6-7 per 100 hectares during the six-year economic plan (1971-76). The programs of mechanization and chemicalization, two of the remaining tasks of the technical revolution in agriculture, are projected to be completed by the end of the current six-year plan period.[38] It is also stressed that the three main goals of technical revolution in the six-year plan period are to reduce the differences between heavy labor and light labor, to close the gap between agricultural and industrial work, and to emancipate women from the heavy burden of household chores, all of which are to be accomplished by 1975.

The cultural revolution is closely linked with the technical revolution. The primary goals of the cultural revolution, therefore, have been the "liberation of the working people from age-old social and spiritual bondage, arming them with the ideology of the working class, and raising their intellectual and spiritual standard of living by enlightening and improving their cultural life through the creation of a new socialist culture."[39] The cultural revolution was, thus, perceived as the essential prerequisite for the socialist revolution and invaluable for the development of socialist society. It was therefore designed to overcome such obstacles to economic and social mobilization as primitive superstitions, family ties sanctioned by Confucian values, and the persistent factionalism caused by local and regional considerations. Because of Korea's specific cultural tradition, contempt for manual labor and low esteem for material values were deeply entrenched in the beliefs and attitudes of the upper middle class, and such practices consequently prevented the educated class from taking an active interest in production work, while the peasants were unwilling to accept the need for continuity and discipline in industrial work. Such habits and attitudes as these had to be changed by some combination of coercion and reeducation, both of which were the primary tasks of the cultural revolution launched as early as 1958.

The centrally planned and directed program of education was also an important part of the cultural revolution, since the education program concentrated on the creation of "a new socialist culture" with drastic changes in the old styles of living and the people's traditional attitudes toward their work. After the liberation in 1945, North Korea had more than 2.3 million illiterates and not a single college or scientific research institute. Therefore, the fundamental task of the cultural revolution was to raise the cultural and technical standards of the working people, who had been recruited for technical work even though they had no primary education. The first task was to educate them. The compulsory education program was introduced in 1950 as a part of the people's educational system; it was raised to the seventh grade in 1958. A free, compulsory education for every school-age child was introduced in 1959. Two and one-half million children, a quarter of the population, were receiving a seven-year education in more than 8500 schools by the end of the five-year plan in 1960.[40] However, by 1967 a program of nine years of compulsory education had been launched, and children in elementary and middle school now receive free education.

The basic policy of education in North Korea has been to establish unity between education and production work. The students acquire knowledge at school, but they must be able to demonstrate their knowledge in practice. They are urged to master the educational philosophy of uniting theory and practice. The ability of a student to integrate knowledge acquired in school into the practical work he performs in society is an important criterion by which the success or failure of the educational system is evaluated. This policy of creating unity between theory and practice served as the main focus of the cultural revolution in the 1960s.

The North Korean leadership also set up "workers' schools" and "workers' middle schools" in the farms and factories in order to educate the illiterates. More than a million workers are reported to have benefited from such programs by learning to read and acquiring at least one technical skill. The government also established a continuing education program to train and educate the newly emerging intelligentsia, a majority of whom were of working class or peasant origin, and also to reeducate the intellectuals of the old educational system so that they might be useful in the construction of socialism in North Korea. In addition, North Korea created more than 78 new colleges and universities, which were able to enroll more than 100,000 students by 1961.

The graduates of such institutions became the key administrators, technocrats, and managers when the seven-year economic plan was being implemented in the 1960s. [41] The number of colleges and universities increased to 130 by 1970, and more than 600, 000 new technicians have been produced, a figure projected to reach one million by the end of the six-year plan in 1975.

The cultural revolution in the countryside was considered a prerequisite for the technical revolution as well as for the building of a new socialist culture, which is to be created by combining nationalistic form with socialistic content. However, there will be strong emphasis on the ideology of chuch'e in every aspect of cultural life. To improve the cultural standard of living, the North Korean leadership established libraries, democratic propaganda rooms, and broadcasting networks in every village and town, all of which function as the key agents of culural change in rural areas.

The cultural revolution, in short,was designed primarily to bring about fundamental change in the ideology and consciousness of the entire people and transform their moral and spiritual values. After a decade of hard work, the North Korean leadership seemed to admit that the task of transforming people's ideology and consciousness is by no means easy, and that it may be a long and arduous process, taking more than a decade or even a whole generation. For this purpose, the ideological revolution was enunciated in the 1960s, but its main thrust was to inculcate Kim's idea of chuch'e in order to eliminate dogmatism, formalism, familism, and the big-power orientation of the people (sadae chui sasang). The ideological remolding of the 1960s combined the program of educating by means of the party's policy directives and the program of inculcating the revolutionary tradition of the 1930s, in which guerrilla-type struggles had been waged persistently for more than a decade and a half. The objective of such programs was to resolve contradictions between the new and old, positiveness and passivity, the idea of continued reform and conservatism, collectivism and individualism. Such an ideological revolution was reported to have created a "new communist man" in the socialist society under the slogan "one for all and all for one." [42] However, the transformation of a people's ideology and consciousness is still an ideal goal rather than a reality, and it may yet take many more decades to reach.

TOWARDS THE HIGHER STAGE OF THE SOCIALIST SYSTEM

In his keynote speech, "Let Us Strengthen the Socialist System of our Country, " before the first session of the Fifth Supreme People's Assembly on December 25, 1972, Kim Il-sung asserted, "The New Socialist Constitution accurately reflects the achievements of the revolution in building socialism in our country." [43] Therefore, the new constitution "defines the principles governing political, economic, and cultural activities in socialist society, " Kim continued, "and the basic rights and duties of the citizens, and stipulates the composition and functions of the state organs and the principles of their activities." In short, the new constitution adopted on December 27, 1972, incorporated President Kim's political thought, the chuch'e idea, with three main components he had expounded in the late 1960s: independence in politics, self-reliance in economy, and self-defense in military affairs.

The drafting of a new constitution in a communist society like North Korea signifies a new definition of the current stage of socialist development. As Andre Vishinsky has explained, the fundamental law of a communist state is not a superstructure, like the constitution in a bourgeois state, but a full reflection of what has been achieved in socialist society. In the late 1960s, when the seven-year economic plan (1961-67) was approaching completion (it was postponed to 1970 at the KWP Conference in October 1966), academicians and theorists in North Korea began to debate two important issues: whether North Korea had already passed the transitional period of socialist revolution and construction, and where the demarcation line for the transitional stage in socialist development was to be drawn.

The first stage of the people's democratic revolution, clearly defined and reflected in the 1948 constitution, came when North Korea embarked on "the antiimperialist, antifeudalistic revolution" after the liberation of Korea from Japanese rule in 1945. This stage in development, as discussed earlier, was characterized by the creation of a state-operated economy and a small scale commodity sector consisting of the private peasant economy in the countryside and the urban handicraft economy in the towns. The people's democracy stage was said to have been completed by 1953, when the North Korean leadership embarked on a new stage to prepare for socialism. The socialist revolution stage was set up by the First Five-Year Economic Plan (1957-61). During this period the agricultural cooperatives were set up, and the socialist reorganization of private trade and individual manufacturing took place with the establishment of producers' cooperatives in small and handicraft industries. The material and technological foundations for socialism were thus established.

After laying the foundation for socialism in the 1950s, North Korea embarked on a new stage in the 1960s; the construction of socialism under the seven-year economic development plan. This development was characterized by North Korea's attempt to mobilize its own domestic resources for economic development following the Soviet failure to either provide ideological unity within the communist bloc or to offer economic aid and technical assistance, which North Korea needed badly to fulfill the seven-year plan. The circumstances that led the North Korean leadership to declare a policy of independence are complex, but 1966 marked the highpoint of Sino-Soviet competition to influence and control development in North Korea. Pressured by both China and *there must be more to it than this...*

the Soviet Union to pick sides in their ideological dispute, the North Korean leadership decided on an independent policy based on Kim's chuch'e idea.

The ideology of chuch'e, expounded by Kim Il-sung as early as 1956, was "to build an independent national economy on the principle of self-reliance" and "to carry out the mass line of the Korean Workers Party and effect the principle of self-defense in national defense to the fullest extent."[44] Kim's idea of chuch'e is now codified in Article 4 of the new constitution, which emphasizes that "the Democratic People's Republic of Korea is guided in its activity by the chuch'e idea of the Workers' Party of Korea which is a creative application of Marxism-Leninism to our country's reality."

Another important aspect of the new constitution is the settlement of the theoretical controversy over the "transitional period" in the socialist stage of development and the role of the "dictatorship of the proletariat" in that period. Disputes over these two issues seem to have taken place in 1967-69, when completion of the seven-year plan was postponed from 1967 to 1970. Academicians and theorists who considered the transition as occurring during the period between capitalism and the victory of socialism seem to have argued that the transitional period in North Korea ended when the seven-year economic plan was fulfilled. This meant, they said, that North Korea had already achieved socialist revolution. Therefore, they talked of ending the dictatorship of the proletariat, giving up the class struggle, and living at peace with imperialism. President Kim charged, however, that they were rightist deviationists, and their views were discredited.

Another group of theorists took the position that the transitional period should be the period between capitalism and the higher stage of communism. The transitional period could not end with the seven-year plan because North Korea had not yet achieved a classless society. Moreover, class distinctions between the workers and the peasants continued to exist after the completion of the seven-year plan. The transitional period could be ended, according to this group, only when there was no distinction between mental and physical labor, when each person worked according to his ability and received payment according to his needs. This group later was charged by Kim Il-sung with being leftist opportunists. Where, then, to draw the demarcation line for the transitional period in the socialist stage of development?

"I deem it right to regard it (the transitional period) as the period up to socialism," President Kim stressed, "but it is wrong to believe that the transition period will come to a close as soon as the socialist revolution is victorious and the socialist system is established."[45] Furthermore, according to this official view, the establishment of the socialist system is not to be misconstrued as the complete victory of socialism. The new constitution proclaims that the socialist system has already been established in North Korea because the exploitative class has been eliminated. However, the victory of socialism has not

19

yet been achieved, because the distinction between the working class and the peasantry continues to exist. Therefore, by executing the triple revolution of technology, culture, and ideology in the 1970s, the North Korean leadership aims at the victory of socialism. Article 25 of the new constitution emphasizes that "the State accelerates the technical revolution to eliminate the distinctions between heavy and light labor and between agricultural and industrial labor, to free the working people from backbreaking labor, and gradually to narrow the difference between physical and mental labor."[46]

For the past quarter-century, industrial development in North Korea has been achieved with exceptionally rapid speed; industrial production is claimed to have increased 38.7 times since 1948.[47] During the period from 1961 to 1970, an average annual growth of 12.8 percent was registered in the industrial output of North Korea. The breakdown of this growth by year is as follows: 14 percent in 1961, 17 percent in 1962, 8 percent in 1963, 17 percent in 1964, and 14 percent in 1965. The figures for 1966-69 have not been made available by the North Korean government. However, during the period of socialist industrialization from 1957 to 1970, industrial production is reported to have increased by an annual average of 19.1 percent. North Korea claims that it achieved the stage of socialist-industrial society by 1970.

In the first half of the present six-year plan, from 1971 to 1973, there was an average annual increase of 17 percent in the industrial output, and this growth was said to have been achieved "under conditions where the production scale expanded 20 times as compared with the early period of industrialization."[48] The value of North Korea's gross industrial output was reportedly 11.6 times that of 1956, and industrial output in 1973 rose 1.6 times that of 1970. In his report to the National Industrial Congress on February 25, 1974, Yon Hyong-muk, a member of the KWP's Central Committee, asserted that "the industrial output of our country in 1973 chalked up a 60 percent gain over 1970 with an average annual growth of 17 percent. Our industry developed faster than in the seven-year plan period, and this high speed of development far surpassed the growth rate envisaged in the six-year plan."[49]

In the rural sector, the growth of agricultural production has not been so impressive as that of the industrial sector, despite the efforts of the North Korean leadership to increase agricultural production ever since the publication of Kim Il-sung's "Theses on the Socialist Rural Question" in February 1964. Private ownership of land, which was implemented by the land reform program of 1946, was gradually socialized, and the cooperative ownership system was introduced in 1958 to encourage rapid increase in agricultural production by collective means. However, cooperative ownership apparently failed to meet the expectations of the leadership to increase productivity and management efficiency; therefore, it was further restructured to create ownership of land by the entire people (meaning state ownership) in 1964.

By introducing the triple revolution of technology, culture, and ideology to the countryside in the 1960s, the North Korean leadership attempted to resolve such agrarian problems as the shortage of technical personnel, inefficiency in cooperative management, and conservative attitudes and behavior on the part of the peasant population. Since rural development was lagging far behind industrial development, industrial workers were urged to go to the rural areas to assist in agricultural production; industry was instructed to supply much-needed machinery, fertilizer, and chemical products to the peasants; and the urban sector was encouraged to render whatever assistance the rural areas needed from towns. [50]

After ten years of efforts to solve the problems of agricultural productivity, the North Korean leadership has not yet entirely succeeded; therefore, it has adopted a policy of concentrating its efforts on the rural technical revolution. In his report to the National Agricultural Congress on January 4, 1974, the chairman of the Agricultural Commission, So Kuang-hi, asserted that "the last ten years following the publication of the rural theses was a decade of creation and innovation in which . . . . the appearance of our countryside radically changed under the red banner of the three revolutions, ideological, technical, and cultural . . . . our countryside was supplied with 2-2.5 tractors for every 100 chongbo (hectares)." Thus, the task of supplying the countryside with 70,000-80,000 tractors, set forth in the theses on the rural question, has not yet been accomplished. [51]

To remedy this situation, Finance Minister Kim Kyong-nyon stated in his report on the state budget of the DPRK for 1974 that "our Party and Government energetically stepped up rural construction last year by appropriating 1.5 times as much money as in the previous year . . . . last year the number of tractors for every 100 chongbo (hectares) reached 2-2.5, and in the plains areas 3-4. Firm material foundations have been laid for applying more than one ton of chemical fertilizer per chongbo in terms of weight and over 200 kilograms in terms of ingredients." [52] Furthermore, President Kim Il-sung added, "irrigation and electrification have been splendidly completed and mechanization and chemicalization are making successful progress in our countryside." Therefore, "the most urgent task confronting us today in the rural technical revolution is that of accelerating and quickly finishing the mechanization and chemicalization of agriculture." [53] So the solution of agricultural problems lies in increasing the production of farm machinery and providing greater quantities of highly efficient chemical fertilizers and agricultural chemicals, which requires a greater investment of the state budget.

The KWP's Central Committee decided at its Eighth Plenum on February 11-13, 1974, that the planned target of the six-year economic plan (1971-76) will be accomplished a year ahead of schedule, so North Korea may be able to celebrate that success on the 30th anniversary of the KWP in October 1975. To scale an even higher peak of the socialist system in the next two years (1974-75), the North Korean leadership has established ten major goals (called kochi or "heights") for economic construction. "We must continue to push forward vigorously and quickly to prepare the groundwork for attaining the following goals: 12 million tons of steel; one million tons of non-ferrous metal; 100 million tons of coal; 50,000 million kwh of electric power; 20 million tons of cement; 100,000 chongbo (hectares) of reclaimed tideland; and 10 million tons of grain," the party's resolution urges. [54]

When these ten goals are accomplished, the North Korean leadership should be able to conclude that "the socialist system of the DPRK is a most advanced and superior social system which make the working people the genuine masters of the state and society and ensures them a happy material and cultural life. The DPRK values most the working masses and respects their personality and rights to the utmost."[55] However, statements like these still remain what Johnson calls "goal culture," not necessarily a description of reality. [56]

NOTES

1. The speech made by President Kim Il-sung on the occasion of the 25th anniversary of the founding of the DPRK may be found in Nodong Sinmun (The Workers Daily), an official newspaper of the Central Committee of the KWP, September 10, 1973.

2. Witae-han Sahoe-chui 10-wol Hyokmyong 40-chunyon Kinyom Nonmunjip (Collection of Essays to Commemorate the 40th Anniversary of the Great October Socialist Revolution) (Pyongyang: Academy of Social Sciences Press, 1957).

3. Sahoe-chui Kich'o Konsol-ul wi-han Choson Nodong-tang ui Kyong che Chong-ch'aek (The Economic Policy of the Korean Workers Party for the Construction of the Foundation of Socialism in Korea) (Pyongyang: Academy of Sciences Press, 1961). The Japanese version of this work was published by Shin Nippon Shu-pan sha in Tokyo in 1962.

4. Uri Nara e so-ui Marx-Lenin chui-ui Sung-li (The Victory of Marxism-Leninism in Our Country) (Pyongyang: The Korean Workers Party Press, 1961).

5. Nam In-hyok, Witae-han Suryong Kim Il-sung tong-chi-ui yongto mit'ae Sungli-han Minchok Haepang Inmin Minchu-chui Hyokmyong Kyongham (The Experience of National Liberation and People's Democratic Revolution under the Leadership of the Great Leader Kim Il-sung) (Pyongyang: Humanistic Sciences Press, 1972).

6. Ibid.

7. Kim Il-sung Sonjip (The Selected Works of Kim Il-sung) (Pyongyang: The Korean Workers Press, 1960), IV, 445.

...uses all NK docs. (—this is one way to do it)

8. See the editorial, "Genuine State of Workers and Peasants," The Pyongyang Times, September 8, 1973.

9. See Nodong Sinmun, September 9, 1973.

10. See Kim Il-sung's speech in October 1945, "On the Construction of North Korea and the National United Front," in Selected Works, op. cit., I, 4.

11. For rich information on the Korean communist movement in general and, more specifically, Kim Il-sung's role in the anti-Japanese armed struggle, see Dae Suk Suh, The Korean Communist Movement, 1918-1948 Princeton, N.J.: Princeton University Press, 1967), and Robert A. Scalapino and Chong-sik Lee, Communism in Korea (Berkeley: University of California Press, 1972), vol. I, The Movement.

12. October 10, 1945, is officially designated by the North Korean communists as the date of the founding of the Korean Workers Party, but the name of the party at the time of the organizational meeting has been invariably recorded as "The North Korean Bureau of the Korean Communist Party's Central Committee" or "The Central Organization Committee of the North Korean Communist Party."

13. The seven-member Politburo, in addition to the chairman (Kim Tu-bong) and two vice chairmen (Kim Il-sung and Chu Yung-ha), included Ch'oe Ch'ang-ik (the Yenan group leader), Ho Ka-yi (the Soviet returned group leader and director of organization), Kim Mu-chong (The Yenan returnee and director of cadre training), and Kim Ch'ang-man (domestic-bred group leader and director of propaganda).

14. The reports and writing dealing with the background of Kim Il-sung, the majority of which were provided by North Korean refugees and South Korean Military Intelligence sources in the late 1940s and 1950s, seem to indicate that Kim was an army major in the Soviet Red Army who was imposed on North Korea as the front of the Soviet occupation forces and served as the stooge of the international communist conspiracy in Korea. These kinds of writings during the cold war era certainly colored the perception and attitudes of the policy makers in Korea and in other parts of the world.

15. See, for example, Hugh Seton-Watson, The East European Revolution (New York: Praeger Publishers, 1951), and Zbigniew K. Brzezinski, The Soviet Bloc: Unity and Conflict (Cambridge, Mass. Harvard University Press, 1960, rev. ed. 1967).

16. Pukhan Ch'ongkam (General Handbook on North Korea) (Seoul: Research Institute on Communist Bloc Problems, 1968), p. 61.

17. Ibid., p. 66. For a more recent explication of the theory, see Kang In-Duk, "The Nature of North Korea's People's Democratic Revolution and Its Policy Implication," in Kang In-Duk, ed., Sege Kongsan-Kwon Ch'ongkam (The General Handbook of World Communist Areas) (Seoul: Research Institute on Far Eastern Affairs, 1972), pp. 793-798.

18. Kim Il-sung Shosaku-shu (Collected Work of Kim Il-sung) (Tokyo: Mirai-sha, 1971), V, 313.

19. Kim Il-sung, "Report of the Central Committee of the Workers' Party of Korea to the Third Congress," April 23, 1956, in Third Congress

of the Workers' Party of Korea: Documents and Materials (Pyongyang: Foreign Languages Publishing House, 1956).

20. Kim Il-sung, Collected Work, op. cit., I, 334.

21. Kim Han-ju, "The October Revolution Brought a Solution to the Problems of Land and Agriculture in Our Country," in Essays on Socialist Revolution, op. cit., p. 161.

22. Ibid.

23. See The Economic Policy of the KWP, op. cit., p. 19.

24. Kim Il-sung, Selected Works, op. cit., V, 289.

25. For an excellent discussion of the cooperative movement, see Robert A. Scalapino and Chong-sik Lee, op. cit., vol. II, The Society.

26. The Economic Policy of the KWP, op. cit., p. 48.

27. Ibid.

28. Ibid., p. 79, for statistical figures on cooperatives from 1953 to 1958.

29. Ibid., p. 38.

30. Ma Ch'un-yong and Ch'oe Chong-hyon, "The Great Upsurge of the Socialist Construction in Our Country," in The Victory of Marxism-Leninism, op. cit., p. 337.

31. Ibid., pp. 344-345.

32. Ibid., p. 345.

33. Quoted in Yi Son-kuk, "The Technical Revolution in Our Country," in The Victory of Marxism-Leninism, op. cit., p. 203.

34. Kim Il-sung, Selected Works, op. cit., VI, 104.

35. See the report of First Vice Premier Kim Il on economic development at the Party Conference of October 5-12, 1966. See Nodong Sinmun, October 7, 1966.

36. See the report of the Fifth Congress of the KWP, November 2-13, 1970, especially Kim Il, "On the Six-Year (1971-76) Plan for the Development of the National Economy of the DPRK," Nodong Sinmum, November 10, 1970.

37. Yi Son-kuk, "The Technical Revolution in Our Country," in The Victory of Marxism-Leninism, op. cit., p. 218.

38. See the proceedings and reports of the National Agricultural Congress, January 4-10, 1974, The Pyongyang Times, January 12, 1974.

39. Kim Song-ki, "The Cultural Revolution in Our Country," in The Victory of Marxism-Leninism, op. cit., p. 116.

40. Ibid., p. 119.

41. Ibid., p. 121.

42. Ibid., p. 125.

43. Kim Il-sung, "Let Us Strengthen the Socialist System of Our Country," in Korea Daily News issued by the Korean Central News Agency (KCNA), in Pyongyang and Tokyo, December 28, 1972, pp. 7-40.

44. Kim Il-sung, "The Present Situation and the Task Confronting Our Party," published by the Central Standing Committee of the General Association of Korean Residents in Japan, October 1966, p. 38.

45. Kim Il-sung, "On the Questions of the Period of Transition from Capitalism to Socialism and the Dictatorship of the Proletariat,"

in Li Yuk-sa, ed., JUCHE: The Speeches and Writing of Kim Il-sung (New York: Grossman Publishers, 1972), p. 117.

46. A full text of the North Korean Constitution may be found in Journal of Korean Affairs (Silver Spring, Md.: Research Institute on Korean Affairs) 2, no. 4 (January 1973) 46-57.

47. For Kim Il's report on the Six-Year Economic Plan, see Nodang Sinmum, November 10, 1970.

48. The Pyongyang Times, April 13, 1974.

49. Yon Hyong-muk, "General Mobilization of All Efforts in Industry to do the Grand Work of Socialist Construction," report to the National Industrial Congress on February 25, 1974, in The People's Korea (Tokyo), March 13, 1974.

50. "Theses on the Socialist Rural Question in Our Country," a speech delivered by Kim Il-sung on February 25, 1964, is in Li Yuk-sa, op. cit., pp. 65-108. In February 1974, to commemorate the 10th anniversary of this speech, a series of articles and commentaries dealing with rural development appeared in The Pyongyang Times and The People's Korea (Tokyo) these seem to provide insight into the agrarian problems of North Korea.

51. So Kwang-hi, "Report to the National Agricultural Congress," January 4, 1974, The Pyongyang Times, January 12. 1974.

52. Kim Kyong-nyon, "On the Review of the Execution of the State Budget for 1973 and the Budget of 1974 of the DPRK," report of the Finance Minister to the Third Session of the Fifth Supreme People's Assembly, March 20-25, 1974, The Pyongyang Times, March 30, 1974.

53. Kim Il-sung, "Let Us Further Consolidate and Develop the Great Successes Achieved in the Building of a Socialist Countryside," speech delivered at the closing session of the National Agricultural Congress on January 10, 1974, The Pyongyang Times, January 26, 1974.

54. See The Pyongyang Times, February 20, 1974.

55. See The Pyongyang Times, February 26, 1974.

56. For Chalmers Johnson's explanation of "goal culture," see "Comparing Communist Nations" in Chalmers Johnson, ed., Change in Communist Systems (Stanford, Calif.: Stanford University Press, 1970), pp. 1-32.

CHAPTER

2

LEADERSHIP
STRUCTURE AND
POLITICAL CULTURE

In the 1970s, in order to cope with the structural changes that had occurred in North Korean society as a result of the socioeconomic development in the 1950s and 1960s, the North Korean leadership began reorganizing the party and the government. Under the 1972 Constitution, power was concentrated in the person of Kim Il-sung and a group of the revolutionary elite who had followed his leadership for more than four decades. Kim Il-sung was elected president of the DPRK in December 1972, the year he celebrated his 60th birthday. The establishment of the presidency represented a process of legitimizing Kim's 25 years of monolithic rule over the North Korean people. He is now the single most powerful leader in the DPRK, for he not only holds the most important positions—president of the DPRK, general secretary of the KWP, and supreme commander of the armed forces—but also exercises the most pervasive authority over all of North Korean society. Thus, Kim's political system has been characterized as an authoritarian oligarchy that has achieved an impressive record of economic development and has succeeded in transforming North Korea's political culture by means of ideological indoctrination and education.

Since political culture plays a very important role in the process of political change and economic development, this chapter will first present a microlevel discussion of Kim's political beliefs and his peculiar style of leadership in the context of the changing characteristics of the power structure, and then a macrolevel analysis of the transformation of North Korea's political culture. Kim Il-sung has persistently attempted to transform traditional political culture, which was based on Confucian ethics, into a new socialist culture embodying his chuch'e idea, in order to create the individual's sense of membership in the larger political community that Kim has been building for the past quarter-century. Since the study of mass political culture depends largely on advanced techniques of survey research and sophisticated methods of measuring public opinion that are not likely to be applied to North Korea, our discussion of North Korean political culture has to be focused on the ways in which the people's orientation toward their political system has been changed to conform to the beliefs, values, and institutions of the ruling elite.

KIM'S STYLES OF LEADERSHIP

The dynamics of the political process in North Korea for the past two and one-half decades have evolved around the development of the leadership styles and techniques of Kim Il-sung and his ruling elite. Observers of North Korean politics have often characterized Kim's regime as a one-man dictatorship or a totalitarian system. It is also said that Kim's tight control of both party and government has a certain resemblance to Stalin's totalitarian method, so he is sometimes portrayed as a little Stalin in the East. [1] However, the development of Kim's leadership styles and techniques in the late 1960s as well as his methods of building organizational authority and control seem to indicate that his methods are quite different from Stalin's.

Having accumulated experience in organizing and leading the anti-Japanese armed struggles in Manchuria for more than a decade and a half beginning in the 1930s, Kim mastered the organizational techniques of iron discipline and persistent and arduous struggle to achieve final victory. However, Kim's personal influence and authority, which now function as the symbol of North Korea's political institutions, were derived from his own ability to organize a hard core of leadership personnel around him and to develop the organizational techniques of unleashing the latent energy and power of the masses. When he was placed in the position of leadership in 1945 by the support of the Soviet military government, he started with a small leadership core who were loyal to him and dedicated to his vision of a desirable society and his prescription for attaining that goal. Had it not been for his leadership skills and organizational techniques, Kim would have been ousted from his position, no matter how strong his Soviet support, in the struggles for power and policy that have recurred in the past quarter-century.

In 1945, when Kim Il-sung appeared on North Korea's political scene, he led only a handful of guerrilla leaders who had been associated with him in Manchuria. The majority of the power elite operating in North Korea were in disarray. They were unable to agree on a single leader around whom to be united, nor had they been able to formulate imaginative programs that would win them the support and loyalty of the population. Kim Il-sung stepped into this political vacuum and organizational chaos in order to build new instituions and formulate new policies to achieve his own vision of a desirable world. The continuity and change in Kim's leadership styles and techniques have been delineated by his colleagues of the anti-Japanese armed struggles who are also members of the Politburo, the policy formulation center.

In April 1972, on the occasion of Kim's 60th birthday, a series of essays and articles were published in the party's newspaper Nodong Sinmun (The Workers' Daily) to commemorate the revolutionary experience. The articles were written by Kim Il-sung's closest associates and most loyal followers from the Manchurian period. All of the contributors are full members of the Politburo of the KWP and hold key offices in the government. They praised Kim's contribution to the development of the Korean revolution and the post-Korean War industrialization as the most important factors in the history of 50 million Korean people. He was, thus, portrayed as the creator of Korea's revolutionary tradition (by Vice Premier Ch'oe Yong-kon); as the founder of the DPRK (by Premier Kim Il); as the genius of the revolution (by First Vice Premier Pak Song-ch'ol); as an invincible military strategist (by Defense Minister Ch'oe Hyon); as a great theorist (by the director of organization and guidance of the KWP's Central Committee, Kim Yong-Chu); as an exceptional leader of the international communist movement (by Director of International Relations Kim Tong-kyu); as the most dedicated initiator and leader of North Korea's reunification policy (by the director of the KWP's southern strategy, Kim Chung-nin); and as a founder and leader of the KWP (by Yang Hyong-sop, who is in charge of social sciences in the Secretariat of the KWP's Central Committee). [2]

These articles, along with a special issue of Korean Affairs Monthly (April 1972) devoted to an exposition of Kim's thought and theory, seem to indicate that the development of Kim's personality cult in North Korea has now reached its fullest extent and may have surpassed that of Stalin in the Soviet Union or that of Mao in China. No living leader in the communist world, with the exception of Mao, is held in such high esteem by his people as Kim is in North Korea. The process of building up Kim Il-sung as the single most powerful leader, founder, and theorist of the DPRK had already begun in the 1950s, when the monolithic communist system was beginning to crumble and the de-Stalinization policy of Nikita Khrushchev encouraged divergent roads to socialism after the 20th Congress of the Communist Party of the Soviet Union in 1956. The impact of policentrism in the international communist movement on the emergence of Kim's personality cult can hardly be denied, because the process was stepped up immediately after Kim's chuch'e idea was enunciated in December 1955, and put into practice beginning in 1956.

After a decade and a half of building Kim's personality cult in North Korea, his followers now recognize him as a "charismatic leader." There is no way of probing the minds of the people and capturing the moods of the society, but Kim's followers see that "powerful results have been accomplished" in the process of economic development and social transformation. Kim's personal mission to make the people's democratic system function, to bring about economic equality and abundance under the socialist industrialization program, and to achieve the reunification of Korea have been closely identified with a sense of public mission. In the course of transforming this personal mission into a public one, Kim

Il-sung has succeeded in shifting his style of leadership from the personal to the institutional.

The traditional political culture was based on Confucian ethics, in which the family was the central socializing element. The traditional political structure relied heavily on the family unit, and the father functioned as an authoritarian figure in the family. The transformation of the cultural and organizational system based on Confucian values and heritage was executed by the cultural revolution, while the remolding of individual personalities was carried out by means of the ideological revolution. Thus, Kim was able to transform an individual's "dutiful respect and filial piety" toward the father of the family into an attitude of "supreme loyalty and total commitment" to the single leader of the country. Kim has now emerged as "the beloved and respected leader-father" of the great family of more than 13 million people in North Korea.

The leadership style of Kim Il-sung, therefore, involves his own methods of managing conflict and violence. For example, in the conflict of 1956-58, when his loyal supporters were divided into two contending factions and engaged in policy disputes (one group advocating North Korea's policy orientation toward the Soviet Union and the other pressuring hard to side with Communist China), Kim Il-sung resolved the differences by enunciating his own idea of chuch'e. "The idea of chuch'e is by no means a theory for the sake of theory," Kim asserted, "but it is rather our own leadership theory by which the policies of revolution and construction have been executed. Therefore, the idea of chuch'e in our country serves as the practical guideline for the solution of problems."[3] The factional problems of the 1950s were, thus, resolved by the application of Kim's chuch'e. However, the leaders of the pro-Soviet faction and the pro-Chinese faction were ruthlessly purged from leadership positions in the party and the governmnet.

Another example of Kim's method of managing conflict and violence was the settlement of the policy conflict of 1966-68, in which a military-led "hard line group" pushed hard to have Kim Il-sung accept a policy of vigilance and a militant posture toward South Korea and American "imperialism." Under this policy line the seizure of the American intelligence ship Pueblo took place, the raid on the presidential palace of South Korea was carried out, and American reconnaissance plane CE121 was shot down. Thus, Kim adopted the militant policy line of the hawkish group by eliminating the moderate group from policy-making positions in the KWP and the government. (A discussion of the policy issues and personalities involved in the controversy is presented in Chapter 4). Having associated with the party and government bureaucracy, the moderate group led by Pak Kum-ch'ol, vice chairman of the Supreme People's Assembly's Standing Committee and Yi Hyo-sun, director of southern strategy in the KWP's Central Committee, were more sympathetic to the revisionistic trends of the Soviet Union and the East European countries.

However, in 1969 Kim reverted to his moderate policy because the policy of vigilance and military operation had not yielded the desired result in 1968. He purged some of the military generals responsible for the failure of the military policy. Moderate leaders like Yim Ch'un-ch'u and Yi Hyo-sun, who had advocated a political solution to the unification problem rather than a military approach, were rehabilitated and placed in positions of leadership in the party and the government.

Another important aspect of Kim's leadership is the application of the concept of "warfare" to all the political and economic activities of North Korea. Kim's rich experience in organizing and leading the anti-Japanese partisan movement in Manchuria in the 1930s and 1940s seems to have hardened his belief that the building of a leadership core and the implementation of iron discipline are two essential principles of any organization if it is going to carry out a persistent and arduous struggle. Thus, in the process of building an organizational structure and establishing leadership techniques in North Korea, Kim has followed the model of the partisan units that he organized and led against the Japanese military occupation in Manchuria. The idea of building a leadership core in every organization is said to have developed as a result of the persistent factionalism in the Korean communist movement in the 1920s, which brought about the expulsion of the Korean communist party from the Communist International (Comintern) in 1928 and ruined the entire movement.

Kim's guerrilla units, based on the organizational principles of core leadership and iron discipline, won battle after battle, according to the official explication, and brought about the final victory of Korean liberation in 1945. [4] Therefore, the revolutionary thought and tradition of Kim's guerrilla units must not only be preserved and applied to the solution of problems arising in political and economic development, but also be inculcated into the entire population, from nursery school children to adults, so that they may live and work like full-fledged members of Kim's guerrilla units. To Kim the task of revolution and economic construction is a kind of warfare; therefore, the society and the people must be organized like an army, with iron discipline and a rigid chain of command. Even production units are patterned after the guerrilla units of Manchurian days, while the workteam functions like a squad in the anti-Japanese armed struggles. "We should train all working people to be honorable Chollima [flying horse] riders," Kim told the workteam movement, "ardent revolutionary fighters who hold the interests of the collective dearer than personal interests and take an active part in socialist and communist construction for the prosperity and development of society as a whole." [5] Thus, in the 1960s, when the seven-year economic development plan was being executed, the whole population was converted into an army. The entire society was militarized in order to carry out economic construction as if it were a huge battlefront. Every factory was a battlefield and every worker a soldier, and a victory was to be won by surpassing the production target.

Many of Kim's followers and colleagues who have associated with him from the days of the anti-Japanese armed struggles in Manchuria still consider him commander-in-chief in every aspect of political life and accord him respect and loyalty as if they were still the battalion, regiment, and division commanders of the guerrilla units. Sometimes they not only perceive themselves as such but also behave like squad or platoon leaders whenever they are assigned to administrative or economic organizations. Thus, as president of the DPRK Kim Il-sung is perceived as the supreme commander of the great guerrilla unit of the government and party bureaucracy, and all ministries, bureaus, and production units are led by his loyal supporters as if they were guerrilla fights in Manchuria. Many of those who were members of Kim's guerrilla units, whose number has been variously reported, have written essays and articles recollecting their experiences under Kim Il-sung's direct leadership. These memoirs shed much light on Kim's style of leadership and the formation of the revolutionary elite in the 1930s and 1940s. [6]

What emerges out of this collection of memoirs by his closest associates is that Kim Il-sung has always shown a profound interest and confidence in the people and that the people therefore reciprocate with loyalty and dedication to him. Kim is, thus, portrayed as the hero of the revolution, achieving victory in every battle and winning the support and trust of the people in every struggle. They won every battle because they were fully immersed in the revolutionary thought of Kim Il-sung and always followed his strategy and directions. Thus, Kim's revolutionary thought and leadership style, originated in Manchuria in the 1930s, were gradually conceptualized as the political thought of the DPRK in the 1950s and 1960s, and were institutionalized as Kim's ideology of chuch'e when the 1972 Constitution was drafted and proclaimed as the fundamental law of the DPRK.

STRUCTURAL CHARACTERISTICS OF PARTY AND GOVERNMENT

North Korea's revolutionary elite continues to hold the most powerful positions in the KWP and in the DPRK, like the revolutionary elite of China under Mao Tse-tung. This group dominates the fifteen-member Politburo, the top policy-making body of the KWP, occupies concurrently the leadership positions in the government, and controls the commanding posts of the North Korean armed forces. Moreover, this revolutionary group, unlike the groups returned from exile in the Soviet Union or China, has maintained cohesive unity and considerable solidarity in its political activities, thus functioning as the core of leadership personnel in North Korean politics.

Some members of this elite group were either dropped from leadership positions or purged from the policy-making organs of the KWP when the party organization was restructured or governmental positions reshuffled during the past quarter-century. However, they were rehabilitated or reappointed to their positions of responsibility because Kim Il-sung believes in the possibility of remolding and transforming human nature. By implementing future-oriented education, combined with ideological indoctrination, on the basis of his experiences in the 1930s and 1940s, and by effectively formulating his own ideas of self-identity and self-reliance developed in the 1950s and 1960s, Kim Il-sung has embarked on the road to the final victory of socialist industrialization and modernization.

The same revolutionary elite that was formed during the anti-Japanese armed struggles in Manchuria in the 1930s emerged as the leadership core of the Korean Workers Party in the late 1940s. This group adopted the platform of the KWP, from its inception in June 1949, which stressed that "it will carry out the struggles of representing and protecting the aspirations and interests of the masses of the working people and of building a strong and prosperous nation state." To achieve this lofty goal, the KWP adopted programs as if they were targets in a battlefield and launched attacks on them. The ultimate goals of their program were to build a democratic and independent state by setting up the People's Republic, in which the people would exercise their sovereign rights through the institution of people's committees at each level, and also to create a new social and economic system by transforming the existing economic and social structure so that the masses would benefit from the change. As the vanguard of the working people, the revolutionary elite defined the organizational characteristics of the KWP, a party "representing the aspirations and interests of the Korean people," and declared that the party would be composed of progressive elements drawn from the workers who made a positive commitment to its work of protecting the interests of the working masses.

The party's action program, adopted by the Fourth Congress in September 1961, stressed the maintenance of the party's purity by rejecting any form of revisionism or dogmatism in its application of the general principles of Marxism-Leninism to the specific conditions of Korea; the preservation of the revolutionary tradition acquired in the anti-Japanese armed struggles; and the attainment of a complete victory of socialism in North Korea. [7] Included in this program were both the policy of reunification of the two Koreas under the united front strategy and the promotion of the unity and solidarity of the socialist states by increased education of the party members and working masses with the spirit of proletarian internationalism.

The post-Korean War development of the party structure has been

greatly influenced by two important organizational principles: democratic centralism and collective leadership. The principle of democratic centralism means that the leaders of the higher party echelons
are to be elected by the lower party echelons, and that the elected
leaders of the higher organs are responsible for making regular reports
on their party work to the organs that elected them. This principle also
stipulates that the whole membership is accountable to the entire party
organization, the minority to the majority, the lower echelons to the
higher echelons, and every party unit to the Central Committee of the
KWP. It is also the duty and obligation of the lower party units to
implement the policy decisions and directives of the higher party organs,
while the higher echelons are responsible for the guidance and supervision of work performed by the lower party organs. The principle of
collective leadership, on the other hand, is to be practiced in the party
committees at every level, and the party committee based on collective
leadership is to function as the supreme leadership organ and commanding staff of the party organization at all levels.[8]

Structural changes have occurred in the organization of the KWP
during its quarter-century of development, from the First Congress of
August 1946 to the Fifth Congress of November 1970. The growth of
the party membership from only 4 percent (366,000) of the population
in 1946 to an impressive 11.43 percent (1.6 million) of the total population in 1970 signifies that the North Korean party has now become a
mass political party, eradicating the image of elitism. Table 2.1 shows
the growth of party membership, the ratio of membership to the population,
the composition of the party delegations to each party congress, and the
number of the Central Committee elected by each party congress between
1946 and 1970.

Extraordinary conferences of the KWP's delegates were convened
in March 1958 and October 1966, the two important times when the shift
in North Korean policy took shape. The first conference was held on
March 3-6, 1958, to discuss specifically such policy issues as the
five-year economic plan (1957-61), the party's unity and solidarity,
and the party's organizational structure. It was during the 1956-58
period that the KWP's economic policy of giving priority to heavy industry was criticized and the leadership of Kim Il-sung was challenged;
a full discussion of this period is presented in Chapter 4. Against the
background of the de-Stalinization process in the Soviet Union, a certain element of the North Korean leadership seems to have pressed
hard for the liberalization of economic and social control in North Korea
and the establishment of a collective leadership to replace the one-man

33

TABLE 2.1

The Congress of the KWP (1946-1970)

Congresses and Dates	Membership and Ratio	Composition of Delegations		Number of the CC
I. Aug. 29-30, 1946	366,000 (4 percent)	Not available		
II. March 27-30, 1948	750,000 (8 percent)	Total delegates: Workers: Peasants: Functionaries: Others: Absentees:	999 466 270 234 29 9	87 (67 regular & 20 alternates)
III. April 23-29, 1956	1,164,945 (10 percent)	Total delegates: Workers: Peasants: Functionaries: Others: Absentees:	916 439 192 246 39 2	116 (71 regular & 45 alternates)
IV. Sept. 11-18, 1961	1,311,563 (12.2 percent)	Total delegates: Workers: Peasants: Functionaries: Others: Absentees:	1,657 944 451 191 71 3	135 (85 regular & 50 alternates)
V. Nov. 2-13, 1970	1,600,000 (11.43 percent)	Total delegates: (no breakdown)	1,871	172 (117 regular & 55 alternates)

dictatorship of Kim Il-sung. This struggle for power was carried out within the party's central apparatus by a number of powerful leaders who represented the divergent views of the various factional groupings.

Also during this period, Kim Il-sung was beginning to shift from reliance on the Soviet Union and Communist China to a policy of self-reliance by enunciating his idea of chuch'e. The party conference was called to rationalize the new policy line and step up ideological indoctrination based on Kim's chuch'e idea, and also to introduce the new policy of self-reliance into the programs of economic development and industrialization. Following this conference the leading members of the Soviet-oriented group and the Chinese-returned group, who seem to have argued for a continued orientation toward the two communist giants and counted on their support and assistance, were purged from the party's leadership positions, and Kim's own loyal supporters took full control of the party's policy-making organs. The fifteen-member standing committee (Politburo) of the KWP Central Committee, which was elected by the Third Congress in April 1956, was represented by the leaders of divergent groups operating in the party machinery for nearly a decade. However, following the First Party Conference of March 1958, the leaders of the Soviet faction and the Yenan group were being eliminated and Kim's loyal supporters from Manchurian days were beginning to take control of the Politburo.

The Second Party Conference of October 1966 was also convened at a most critical time in party history, because the completion date of the seven-year economic plan (1961-67) had to be postponed to 1970 and a new policy line of independence in politics, self-reliance in economy, and self-defense in military affairs had to be adopted. Faced with the increasing polemics and ideological conflicts between the Soviet Union and Communist China, Kim Il-sung was forced into taking an independent policy line. "We shall not take any side," Kim asserted. "Should anyone ask us which 'side' we are on, we would answer we are on the 'side' of Marxism, on the 'side' of the revolution. Communists should not be too inquisitive about that."[9] To take an independent policy position in the Sino-Soviet conflict meant that the North Korean leadership was to follow the twin goals of "economic construction" on the one hand and "defense fortification" on the other. This policy of increasing defense expenditures at the expense of economic development brought about a split in the party's leadership, which aggravated the disputes over the choice of policy lines. The outcome of the Second Party Conference clearly indicated that disputes over the policy choice were far from resolved and that changes in North Korea's leadership were forthcoming.

As part of the party's reorganization, the 6-member standing committee of the Politburo was newly created after the party conference. It was composed of Kim Il-sung, Ch'oe Yong-kon, Kim Il, Pak Song-ch'ol, Yi Hyo-sun, and Kim Kwang-hyop. This conference also created the post of General Secretary in the 11-member Secretariat. Kim Il-sung was elected to this post, whereupon he relinquished his chairmanship

of the party's Central Committee. The Secretariat was set up parallel
to the 29-member Politburo of the KWP. The party's top leadership held
interlocking positions in both the Secretariat and the Politburo, which
included Kim Il-sung, Ch'oe Yong-kon, Kim Il, Pak Kum-ch'ol, Yi Hyo-sun,
Kim Kwang-hyop, Sok San, Ho Pong-hak, Kim Yong-chu, and Pak Yong-
kuk. [10] However, following the 15th Plenum of the KWP's Central Committee in March 1967, the key leaders of the moderate faction like Pak
Kum-ch'ol, Kim To-man, and Pak Yong-kuk, along with three Politburo
members (Yi Hyo-sun, Kim Ch'ang-man, and Im Ch'un-ch'u) were purged
from their leadership positions because of their persistent criticism and
challenges to the policy of expanding the defense buildup at the expense
of sustained economic development.

The policy perspectives of the moderate faction were representative
of those government bureaucrats, economic managers, and technocrats
who were increasingly concerned with developing a rational economic
policy for industrialization and modernization. The hawkish faction,
including the military leaders like Ho Pong-hak, Sok San, and Kim
Ch'ang-pong, on the other hand, pushed very hard to have Kim Il-sung
accept a militant policy posture toward South Korea and American "imperialism," accompanied by an increased defense buildup. In this conflict,
the hard-line military policy seems to have prevailed over the moderate
economic policy, since the North Korean government increased the
defense budget to nearly 30 percent and stepped up the fortification of
defense facilities.

However, the outcome of this policy line was in many respects
counterproductive, since the South Korean government had also increased
its defense posture under the new program of modernization supported
by the United States. North Korea's militant policy line had also aroused
the Japanese ruling elite, who considered the security of South Korea to
be directly connected with their own. This awareness subsequently produced a clause in the Nixon-Sato Joint Communique that the security of
South Korea is essential to the security of Japan. When the militant
policy posture failed to yield the desired result, the key members of the
hawkish faction, Ho Pong-hak, Kim Ch'ang-pong, and Ch'oe Kwang,
all five-star generals, along with other senior military officers, were
purged from their leadership positions following the fourth party conference of the Korean People's Army in January 1969.

It was speculated at that time that one of the reasons why the generals were purged and the hard-line policy was shifted to a moderate one
in 1969 was Defense Minister Kim Ch'ang-pong's failure to obtain Soviet
military aid. In June 1966, several months before the convening of the
Second Party Conference, Kim Ch'ang-pong led a military delegation to
Moscow to negotiate the procurement of urgently needed weapons and the
modernization of vital equipment. However, the defense minister returned
home empty-handed, while Vice Premier in charge of Economic Affairs
Yi Chu-yon succeeded in reaching an agreement with the Soviet leaders
to conclude a treaty of economic, scientific, and technical assistance

for the 1967-70 period. Therefore, Defense Minister Kim Ch'ang-pong, supported by his general chief of staff (Ho Pong-hak) and the commanding general of the air force (Ch'oe Kwang), pushed hard to have Kim Il-sung adopt a military strategy based on the policy of independence and self-reliance. Under this policy line the entire population was to be mobilized, the whole country was to be fortified, and the people were to be armed with small weapons. [11] However, this policy line was terminated when Kim Ch'ang-pong, Ho Pong-hak, and Ch'oe Kwang were replaced by such moderate military officers as Ch'oe Hyon as defense minister, O Chin-u as general chief of staff in the army, and Han Ik-su as vice minister of defense, all of whom are also regular members of the Party Politburo.

The new leadership of the KWP, elected by the Fifth Congress in November 1970, included the 15-member Politburo, of which 11 were regular members and 4 were alternates. [12] Parallel to the Politburo, the 10-member Secretariat of the KWP Central Committee was set up, and the number of those who held interlocking positions in both Politburo and Secretariat was narrowed down to only 10: Kim Il-sung, Ch'oe Yong-kon, Kim Il, Kim Yong-chu, O Chin-u, Kim Tong-kyu, Kim Chung-nin, Han Ik-su, Hyon Mu-kwang, and Yang Hyong-sop. They are considered the most influential policy makers and perhaps the closest colleagues of Kim Il-sung in North Korean politics. A brief analysis of these top 10 leaders indicates that all of them have had a lifelong association with Kim Il-sung and that their average age is in the mid-50s, with the exception of President Kim's right hand-man, Vice-President Ch'oe Yong-kon, who reached retirement age in 1972 at 70. Four regular and two alternate members of the Politburo are in their 60s and will probably retire in the 1970s.

Of the 11 regular members of the Politburo, 4—Ch'oe Hyon, minister of defense; O Chin-u, chief of general staff; Han Ik-su, director general of the Political Bureau in the Korean People's Army; and So Ch'ol, former director general of the Political Bureau in the Korean People's Army—represent the interests and aspirations of the military establishment, though they have been considered leaders of the moderate group in the army. Two members, Kim Yong-chu and Kim Tong-kyu, are considered representatives of the younger generation in the KWP; they are in their late 40s and early 50s. The remaining four members are also regarded as representing the moderate group within the party, since their policy perspectives and positions have been antithetical to the hard-line policies led by the militantly hawkish group. This group is said to have pushed the reunification policy that led the North-South Joint Communique of July 4, 1972.

The size of the Politburo was reduced from 26 to 15 and that of the Secretariat from 12 to 10 after the Fifth Congress in order to comply with the policy of decentralization. This policy was also instituted in the executive branch of government when the central government was reor-anized under the 1972 Constitution. Furthermore, the 1970 expansion

of the party's Central Committee from 135 to 172, of which 117 are
regular members and 55 are alternate members, was a good example of
increased participation on the part of a new and younger generation of
local party leaders. Of the 172 members of the Central Committee,
118 (approximately 60 percent) were newly elected, indicating a drastic
change in the composition of the party leadership as well as the severity
of the struggles for power and policy in the 1966-69 period. Only four
members were elected to a fourth term, while six members were elected
to a third term on the KWP Central Committee.

Structural changes in the governmental system also paralleled the
changes in the structure of the KWP when the North Korean leadership
adopted the new socialist constitution in December 1972. The Central
Committee of the KWP decided in October 1972 to establish a commission
to draft a new constitution for the DPRK. Constituent members of the
Fifth Supreme People's Assembly (SPA), elected on December 12, ratified
the new constitution at their first session on December 27, replacing the
1948 constitution, in force for nearly a quarter-century. The 541-member
Supreme People's Assembly, the legislative body for North Korea, was
elected from 541 electoral districts, one deputy for every 30,000 people.[13]

The changes in the composition of the Fifth SPA directly reflected
the drastic changes that took place in the socioeconomic structure, the
party, and the government institutions. A breakdown of the 541-member
assembly by social background shows that 347 were of working class
origin, 72 were of peasant origin, and 122 represented the clerical
workers in the party and government agencies. If we compare the results
of this election with those of the Fourth Supreme People's Assembly,
elected in November 1967, we find an increase of 84 deputies (from 457
in 1967 to 541 in 1972). Three hundred forty-five deputies (63.8 percent)
were newly elected. Only 11 deputies, including Kim Il-sung, Ch'oe
Yong-kon, and Kim Il, were elected for a fifth consecutive term, which
meant a service of nearly a quarter-century since the first election in
August 1948, and 19 deputies were elected for a fourth consecutive term
since the second election in August 1957. Furthermore, the number of
deputies representing the industrial workers and administrators in the
governmental agencies has now increased considerably, thus reducing
the number of deputies representing the peasantry.[14]

Commenting on the constitutional changes that took place at the
first session of the Fifth SPA, Nodong Sinmun asserted that "our
socialist constitution is a true model of a great code for the working
class."[15] In contrast to the 1948 constitution, which accepted the
Stalinist model of government, the socialist constitution of 1972 indicates a synthesis of the constitutional models of the socialist countries
and the domestic need to cope with socioeconomic development. North
Korea has now made a transition from the people's democratic stage of
revolution to the stage of socialist construction, in which the dictatorship of the proletariat is still necessary, as in the constitution of the
People's Republic of China.[16] The new constitution, unlike the old one,

codified the independent policy line of North Korea by stipulating that its policies are formulated on the basis of Kim's ideology of chuch'e. The peaceful approach to the solution of the country's reunification problem is specified in Article 5 of the new constitution, and the complete victory of socialism is predicted only for the northern half of Korea.

Structural changes in the government under the new constitution brought about a concentration and consolidation of political power in the new office of the president (chu-sok) of the DPRK. "The President of the Democratic People's Republic of Korea is the head of state and represents the state power of the DPRK" (Article 89). The duties of the president during his four-year tenure are to provide leadership to the Central People's Committee (CPC), whose functions are defined in Chapter 7 and to convene and preside over the State Administration Council—the cabinet—consisting of the premier, vice premiers, and ministers (Articles 107-108). The president also functions as the supreme commander of all armed forces and the National Defense Commission (Articles 92-93). Under the 1948 constitution, the functions of the head of state were performed by the chairman of the Standing Committee of the Supreme People's Assembly. But under the new constitution, the symbolic functions of the head of state and the actual exercise of political power are combined to give more power to the office of the president. Kim Il-sung was elected as the first president of the DPRK by the Supreme People's Assembly on December 28, 1972, a day after the adoption of the new constitution.

An institutional change in the structure of the central government was the establishment of the 25-member Central People's Committee (CPC). President Kim had said earlier that the underlying purpose of setting up the CPC at the central government level and the people's committees at each local government level was "to perform the function of exercising day-to-day supervision and control over the latter's (administrative bodies') activities so that the administrative bodies are able to do away with bureaucracy in their work and be better servants to the people."[17] The people's committees at all levels, therefore, are to be composed of representatives of the workers, soldiers, and working intellectuals. The 25-member CPC is now headed by President Kim Il-sung. Two vice presidents (Ch'oe Yong-kon and Kang Yang-uk) and a secretary (Yim Ch'un-ch'u) serve, along with 21 other members, all of whom were elected by the first session of the Supreme People's Assembly on December 28, 1972.[18]

The new central government, unlike the old one under the 1948 constitution, separates policy-making functions performed by the Central People's Committee from the policy-execution functions to be carried out by the Central Administration Council. Under the old system, these functions were combined and performed by a single unit, the cabinet (Articles 52-57 of the 1948 Constitution). The CPC has the authority to establish and abolish ministries or executive branches of the government as well as to appoint or dismiss vice premiers, ministers, and other members of the State Administration Council (Article 102). The CPC was, therefore, created specifically to control and supervise the state bureaucracy, whose performance and efficiency were of concern to Kim Il-sung in the 1960s. The control of the CPC over the administrative organizations is repeated at each level of local government, from province down to county, through people's committees elected by the local people's assemblies (see Chapter 9). The policy of popular control of the state bureaucracy through the "people's assembly" had its origin in the Soviet Union, where Lenin developed a key institution, the "soviet" (council).

The State Administrative Council, as an executive organ of the North Korean government, is completely subservient to the direction and administrative guidance of the President and the Central People's Committee. The Council is composed of the newly elected premier, Kim Il; 6 vice premiers: Pak Song-ch'ol, Chong Chun-taek, Kim Man-kom, Ch'oe Chae-u, Nam Il, and Hong Won-kil; the chairmen of 7 commissions: State Planning, Heavy Industry, Machine-Building Industry, Light Industry, Agriculture, Transport and Communication Service to the People; and 15 ministers, all of whom are appointed by the Central People's Committee. The structure of the new cabinet indicates that the central ministries have been reduced by more than half, from 32 to 15, and have been consolidated into larger units, with several ministries combined to create the 7 commissions. For example, the newly created commissions of Heavy Industry, Machine-Building Industry, and Light Industry seem to have absorbed such ministries as the First, Second and Third Ministries of Machine Industry, the Ministries of the Electric and Coal Industry, Metal Industry, Mining Industry, and Textile and Papermaking Industry. The five vice premiers serve as chairmen of the commissions. The reduction in the number of cabinet ministries is a clear indication of administrative decentralization under the new constitution.[19]

The new central government structure, unlike the old, consists of three pillars of power: the Central People's Committee (which is basically a control and supervisory organ), the State Administrative Council (which executes the KWP's policy), and the Standing Committee of the Supreme People's Assembly (a symbolic and honorary body that functions as a legislative unit), all of which are coordinated and directed by the president. One of the most striking characteristics of this new structure is the careful balancing of power based on the concept of collective leadership. A close study of the 19-member Standing Committee of the Supreme People's Assembly indicates that it has no real power in the decision-making processes but is, rather, an honorary representative unit of government organization.

The most important factor in the new structure of the government is the triangular relationship established between the three key institutions of North Korea: the Political Committee (Politburo of the KWP), the Central People's Committee, and the Central Administrative Council. About a dozen key members of the party's Politburo maintain interlocking positions in these institutions, characterizing the power relationship in North Korea. [20] Fourteen of the 16 Politburo members (all except So Ch'ol and Han Ik-su) are represented on the Central People's Committee, while 13 of the 25 CPC members have taken over cabinet posts in the 22-member Central Administrative Council. The close relationship between the party's decision-making organ and the government's policy-making and policy-execution agencies seems to have been designed to provide more efficiency in the management and operation of economic and government organizations.

It might appear that the new governmental system is nothing but an instrument of policy execution for the KWP. However, the CPC has acquired considerable power to make policy in government and economic organizations. But since there is no evidence to support the hypothesis that either the government or the economic bureaucracy helps make policy, it may be said that under the new constitution the North Korean government is still highly centralized.

The new constitution of the DPRK, unlike the draft constitution of the People's Republic of China, did not write in the name of Kim Il-sung as head of state, nor, did it specify any other person to succeed him. Like the constitutions of other Marxian socialist states of Eastern Europe, the North Korean constitution created only institutions and left the choice of individuals to fill the offices to the Supreme People's Assembly, basically the representative body of the entire population. In order to create a strong sense of participation by the people in the political process, the new basic law of North Korea called for strengthening of the key institutions, the people's committees at every level, and their separation from the administrative committees at each level. This concept was devised to maintain a check and balance between the policy-making functions and the policy-execution functions of the new government.

TRANSFORMATION OF POLITICAL CULTURE

The new socialist culture that President Kim would like to see emerge in North Korea as a result of his triple revolution of technology, ideology, and culture is quite similar to Western ideas of modernization and development. The new socialist culture includes a major emphasis on the advancement of science, a need for sophisticated technology, and an accumulation of material resources for progress toward modernity. The goal of ideological revolution, therefore, is to create a new culture based on monolithic ideology by the process of what Gabriel Almond would call "homogeneous socialization." The efforts made by the North Korean leadership to bring about a cultural revolution are closely linked with the tasks of the ideological revolution, since they involve complete changes of attitudes, beliefs, behavioral patterns, and institutions that the North Korean people have inherited from their ancestors.

It is therefore necessary to understand the emerging new culture in
North Korea as a function of politics.

How did the North Korean leadership attempt to creat a new culture? The process of cultural and ideological transformation during
the past quarter-century may be conveniently divided into three phases.
The first phase covers the period of democratic reforms (1945-53),
during which the concept of nation building was fostered and inculcated
among the population. In the second phase, from 1954 to 1958, mass
political education coupled with the indoctrination of class consciousness accompanied the process of agricultural collectivization and
socialist industrialization under the first five-year economic plan.
The third phase covered a whole decade, 1959 to 1970, during which
the cultural and ideological revolutions were stepped up and education
programs of communist ideology were developed throughout the country.[21]

In order to educate the people in a new concept of nation building
in the first phase of ideological transformation, more specific programs
were designed to help them develop a sense of national identity based
on the united front policy. By eradicating age-old traditions and eliminating outmoded thought patterns, including remnants of pro-Japanese
attitudes, from the entire populations, the North Korean leadership
educated the people with such ideas as "patriotic democracy" and
"antiimperialism" so that they could identify themselves as masters
of the emerging new nation. They developed a proud sense of direct
participation in the great cause of building the nation-state. [22]

Therefore, new political institutions like the people's assembly,
the people's committee, and other mass organizations were created
immediately after the liberation to replace the old institutions and also
to implement the programs of ideological education. The tasks of ideological education were to provide the rationale for the execution of such
democratic reforms as redistribution of land, nationalization of industry,
and liberation of women from the chores of housework—they succeeded
in persuading the population that a majority of the people are actually
benefiting from the reform programs. Indeed, the principle of democracy
was used to benefit a majority of the landless, the poor peasants, and
the workers, but dictatorship was imposed on a minority of landlords
and so-called "compradore capitalists."

The transformation of political culture in the second phase was
accomplished by means of a mass political movement throughout the
country. It was during the 1954-58 period that the socialist transformation under the policies of agricultural collectivization and socialization of all private commerce and industry was completed and the
foundation of socialist construction was said to have been laid.
In order to cope with drastic social and economic changes, the North
Korean leadership stepped up its programs of mass political education.
The fundamental task of these programs was to create "a new man in
socialist society by molding and remolding each individual." Therefore,
the KWP "carried out intensive communist education among the masses,

combining it with education in the revolutionary tradition." Kim Il-sung summed it up as follows: "Since the masses have accepted the Party policy of educating and remolding all people, the transformation of men has been taken over by the masses themselves and has been linked more closely with their productive activities."[23]

It was also during this stage of development that Kim Il-sung enunciated his own concept of chuch'e, which was to guide and direct the processes of policy formulation and policy execution. The policy of self-reliance was implemented in such mass political action as the Chollima movement, the Chollima workteam movement, and the education movement. But, Kim's domestic policy of self-reliance and independence was a direct response to such changes in the international environment as the de-Stalinization policy of Nikita Khruschev and the trends of liberalization and policentrism in the Soviet Union and other socialist countries. "Those from the Soviet Union insisted upon the Soviet method and those from China stuck to the Chinese method. So they quarreled, some advocating the Soviet fashion and others the Chinese way." Kim denounced the imitation of foreign methods: "There can be no set rule that we must follow the Soviet pattern. Some advocate the Soviet way and others the Chinese, but is it not high time to work out our own?"[24]

Kim's chuch'e idea, in a nutshell, means that the people are the masters of the Korean revolution and of the building of the socialist system, and that the masses are to function as the motivating force of revolution and construction. "It is the idea that one is responsible for one's own destiny," Kim asserted, "and that one also has the capacity to hew out that destiny."[25] What Kim has emphasized in his writings and speeches for the past decade and a half is that the masses of people, if their political consciousness were fully aroused and their creative wisdom and productive energies were unleashed, could function as the dynamic force of revolution and socialist construction. According to his own interpretation, the policy of self-reliance has enabled North Korea to transform the economic and social structure as well as to achieve success in the programs of socialist industrialization, which might otherwise have taken many more generations or even a century. "Our party has always been victorious because it believed in the strength of the popular masses and gave full play to their revolutionary zeal and creative activity," Kim asserted, "thus encouraging them to use all potentialities and reserves to the full by themselves and to solve all problems arising in revolution and construction according to our actual need."[26]

The inculcation of Kim's chuch'e idea throughout North Korea, beginning in 1956, should be understood and analyzed in the broad context of his leadership techniques. Kim was able to establish himself as the undisputed ruler of North Korea and muster the loyal support of his own oligarchs when he defeated the challenges of the Soviet-returned faction and the Chinese-oriented Yenan group in 1956. Up until the outbreak of the Korean War, Kim accommodated various factional elements to maintain a facade of collective leadership under the united front policy. But the death of Stalin and the de-Stalinization policy brought about a new political environment in which Kim was able to crush any criticism or challenge to his policy. He began to tighten his own control over the party and the government. Kim's chuch'e idea was, thus, utilized as the means to rationalize the process of concentrating authority and power in his own hands. Kim devoted a full decade (1956-66) to the conceptualization of chuch'e, by which his authority and power have been built up to such an extent that he is now called "the most beloved and respected leader and an invincible theorist of revolution" in North Korea.

In the process of conceptualizing chuch'e, Kim has delivered more than a dozen speeches in order to delineate his thought to the propaganda and pedagogical cadres for wide dissemination. The indoctrination programs of communist ideology, combined with education in the anti-Japanese revolutionary tradition, were the most important means of fostering the new political culture based on chuch'e. The processes of ideological remolding were concerned primarily with the establishment of a communist world view, the development of a new communist man, and technical education for the construction of a new socialist society in North Korea. Kim's speech "On Communist Education," therefore, stipulated the following six tasks to be performed by his instructional cadres: (1) to educate the people to the superiority of socialism and communism over capitalism: (2) to make the people recognize that the future will prevail over the past; (3) to have the people eradicate individualism and selfishness, since they are great obstacles to any socialist transformation of a society; (4) to educate the people in socialist patriotism and proletarian internationalism; (5) to cultivate the spirit of love for work among the people; and (6) to educate the people with the revolutionary ideology of uninterrupted revolution and continued reforms for progress. [27]

Education in the revolutionary tradition was designed to circulate widely the record of Kim's anti-Japanese armed struggles in the 1930s and 1940s in order to show the people that Kim and his loyal associates were the most active and important group in the history of Korea's independence movement. Accordingly, the six-volume Memoirs of the Participants in the Anti-Japanese Partisan Movement was compiled and published to spread the story of Kim's heroic leadership in the independence movement and his brilliant military strategy in battle after battle. The essential point of these stories is that "no matter how difficult a situation Kim Il-sung confronted in his armed struggles, he was always able to achieve final victory because of his resilience and persistence"; therefore, if the people emulate Kim's style of leadership and activities in their production work, the final victory of socialist industrialization will be achieved. "Education in communist ideology is a complex task of transforming the people's old patterns of thought and behavior into a new socialist culture, "the party journal admitted. "Therefore, the goal may not be achieved in a generation. However, the party's correct policy of linking the education program of communist ideology and the program of teaching about the revolution should be put into practice in our daily life."[28]

The North Korean leadership, thus, attempted to elicit positive responses from the masses of people by presenting models of heroes and their success stories. But there is no means of confirming or measuring the positive responses the North Korean leadership claims to have evoked from the people. "By educating the party members and the working people with examples of the glorious revolutionary tradition, we not only transformed their thought and behavior but also convinced them of the true existence of the party's revolutionary tradition," a party journal, Kulloja (The Workers), claimed. "Therefore, education in the revolutionary tradition means making the people love our party led by Comrade Kim Il-sung, preserving our revolutionary heritage, and putting party policies into practice in our daily living."[29]

Kim's idea of chuch'e was further refined in the 1960s. He made it explicit in his report to the Fifth Party Congress in November 1970, and gradually institutionalized it as Kim Ilsung-chui ("Kim Ilsungism") in the 1970s. In an article to commemorate Kim's sixtieth birthday in April 1972, "The Great Leader Kim Il-sung is the Originator of Our Party's Revolutionary Tradition," Ch'oe Yong-kon, chairman of the SPA's Standing Committee, said that chuch'e has now been institutionalized as the monolithic ideology (yuil sasang) of the party, the government, and the people of North Korea, because "we have now inherited the revolutionary tradition, which means that we have accepted the ideological system of the anti-Japanese guerrilla units and applied their method and style of work to solve our problems of revolution and construction."[30]

However, the process of institutionalizing revolution based on chuch'e had already begun in 1966, when Nodong Sinmun published an editorial entitled "Let Us Defend Our Independence!" and when Kim Il-sung further delineated the concept in his speech "Let Us Embody the Revolutionary Spirit of Independence, Self-Reliance, and Self-Defense More Thoroughly in All Fields of State Activities" to the Supreme People's Assembly on December 16, 1967. This speech later formed the basis of the ten-point program of the DPRK. Kim's chuch'e idea is based on his revolutionary thought over several decades, one seasoned observer concludes, because it performs a number of interrelated functions, both manifest and latent. On the manifest level it serves to legitimize Kim's political control, to generate a sense of patriotic nationalism, and to foster a sense of participation in the great cause of building a nation-state.[31]

By 1972, chuch'e had been transformed into a new political culture, according to Nodong Sinmun, replacing the traditional political culture based on Confucian ethics, and it has now become "the guiding compass for carrying on successfully our revolution and construction in the decade to come.[32] In the absence of a systematic survey, there is no way of confirming the success of North Korea's attempt to transform the traditional political culture into a new socialist culture. However, the primary function of chuch'e has been the building of strong political institutions, including Kim's personality cult, which have gained respect from their capacity to satisfy the people's political aspirations.

NOTES

1. See Chong-sik Lee, "Stalinism in the East," in Robert A. Scalapino, ed., The Communist Revolution in Asia (Englewood Cliffs, N.J.: Prentice-Hall, Inc., 1965), pp. 114-137.

2. These articles appeared in Nodong Sinmun (The Workers Daily) between April 1 and April 23, 1972. The Japanese translation of these articles appeared in Chosen Shiryo (The Korean Affairs Monthly) (Tokyo: Korean Affairs Institute), 12, no. 5 (May 1972).

3. Kim Il-sung, "On Some Problems of Our party's Chuch'e Idea and the Government of the Republic's Internal and External Policies," Mainichi Shimbun, September 17, 1972.

4. Ch'oe Yong-kon, "The Great Leader Kim Il-sung Is the Originator of Our Party's Glorious Tradition of the Revolution," Nodong Sinmun, April 7, 1972. The founding date of the anti-Japanese guerrilla unit in Manchuria is listed as April 25, 1932.

5. Kim Il-sung, "Let Us Develop the Chollima Workteam Movement in Depth," in Kim Il-sung Sonjip (The Selected Works of Kim Il-sung) (Pyongyang: The Korean Workers Press, 1960), V, 56.

6. See, for example, Chosen Inmin ui Jayu wa Haepang (The Freedom and Liberation of the Korean People): Records of the Anti-Japanese Armed Struggles, compiled by the KWP's Institute of Party History, p. 470. The Japanese version of this volume was published by Miraisha in Tokyo in 1972.

7. See Documents of the Fourth Congress of the Workers' Party of Korea (Pyongyang: Foreign Languages Publishing House, 1961).

8. See Articles 17 and 18 of the Party Statute.

9. Kim Il-sung, "The Present Situation and Our Party's Task," report to the Conference of the KWP on October 5, 1966, published by the Central Standing Committee of the General Association of Korean Residents in Japan (Tokyo, 1966), p. 38.

10. The size of the Politburo, following the Fourth Congress in September 1961, was 18. However, it was expanded to 29 (17 regular and 12 alternate members) after the Second Party Conference of October 1966. The lineup of this Politburo was as follows: Kim Il-sung, Ch'oe Yong-kon, Kim Il, Pak Kum-ch'ol, Kim Ch'ang-man, Yi Hyo-sun, Pak Chong-ai, Kim Kwang-hyop, Chong Il-yong, Nam Il, Yi Chong-ok, Yi

Chu-yon, Kim Ik-son, Kim Ch'ang-pong, Pak Song-ch'ol, Ch'oe Hyon, and Yi Yong-ho. The alternate members included Ha Ang-ch'on, Han Sang-tu, Hyon Mu-kwang, Sok San, Ho Pong-hak, Ch'oe Kwang, O Chin-u, Yim Ch'un-ch'u, Kim Tong-kyu, Kim Yong-chu, Pak Yong-kuk, and Chang Kyong-pak.

11. See the editorial "Let Us Thoroughly Execute Our Party's Independent Policy Line by Arming the Entire People and by Fortifying the Whole Country," Nodong Sinmun, January 18, 1968. Also see the eyewitness report of the defense fortifications by Wilfred G. Burchett, Again Korea (New York: International Publishers, 1968).

12. The lineup of the 15-member Politburo after the Fifth Party Congress was as follows: full members—Kim Il-sung, Ch'oe Yong-kon, Kim Il, Pak Song-ch'ol, Ch'oe Hyon, Kim Yong-chu, O Chin-u, Kim Tong-kyu, So Ch'ol, Kim Chung-nin, Han Ik-su; alternate members—Hyon Mu-kwang, Chong Chun-taek, Yang Hyong-sop, Kim Man-kum.

13. The results of this election indicate that the population of North Korea has now reached approximately 15 million people.

14. For a detailed analysis of the Fifth Supreme People's Assembly, see Kukje Munje (International Problems), published by the Institute for Far Eastern Studies in Seoul, Korea, 9, 3 (March 1973), 82-101.

15. See the editorial "Outstanding Marxist-Leninist Document Illuminating the Road to Victory of Socialism and Communism with the Ray of the Great Chuch'e Idea," Nodong Sinmun, December 28, 1972.

16. The first article of the draft of the Revised Constitution of the People's Republic of China stressed that "the People's Republic of China is a socialist state of proletarian dictatorship led by the working class (through the Chinese Communist Party) and based on the alliance of workers and peasants."

17. Kim Il-sung, "Let Us Strengthen the Socialist System of Our Country," in Korean Daily News of the Korean Central News Agency (KCNA), published in Tokyo, December 28, 1972, pp. 7-40.

18. The list of members of the Central People's Committee was as follows: Kim Il-sung, Ch'oe Yong-kon, Kang Yang-uk, Kim Il, Pak Song-ch'ol, Ch'oe Hyon, O Chin-u, Kim Tong-kyu, Kim Yong-chu, Kim Chung-nin, Hyon Mu-kwang, Yang Hyong-sop, Chong Chun-t'aek, Kim Man-kum, Yi Gun-mo, Ch'oe Chae-u, Yi Chong-ok, Im Ch'un-ch'u, Yon Hyong-muk, O Tae-pong, Nam Il, Hong Won-kil, Yu Chang-sik, Ho Tam, Kim Pyong-ha.

19. President: Kim Il-sung; vice presidents: Ch'oe Yong-kon and Kang Yang-uk; secretary of the Central People's Committee: Yim Ch'un-ch'u. The Central People's Committee appoints the Administrative Council: premier: Kim Il; vice premiers (6): Pak Song-ch'ol, Chong Chun-t'aek, Kim Man-kum, Ch'oe Chae-u, Nam Il, and Hong Won-kil. Chairman of the State Planning Commission: Ch'oe Chae-u. Minister of the people's armed forces: Ch'oe Hyon; minister of foreign affairs: Ho Tam; minister of public security: Kim Pyong-ha; chairman of the Heavy Industry Commission: Yi Cong-ok; chairman of the Machine-

Building Industry Commisssion: Han Song-yong; minister of chemical industry: Kim Hwan; chairman of the Light Industry Commission: Nam Il; chairman of the Agricultural Commission: Kim Man-kum; chairman of the Transport and Communications Commission: Hyon Mu-kwang; minister of fisheries: Kim Yun-sang; minister of the building materials industry: Mun Pyong-il; chairman of the Commission of Service for the People: Pak Song-ch'ol; minister of education: Kim Sok-ki; minister of culture and art: Yi Chang-son; minister of finance: Kim Kyong-yon; minister of foreign trade: Kye Ung-t'ae; minister of external economic affairs: Kong Chin-t'ae; minister of construction: Pak Im-t'ae; minister of labor administration: Chong Tu-hwan; minister of public health: Yi Nak-pin. The Standing Committee of the SPA: Hwang Chang-yop, Hong Ki-mun, So ch'ol, Han Ik-su, Chon Chang-ch'ol, Pak Sin Dok, Kim Yong-nam, Chong Chun-ki, Yum T'ae-chun, Kim Song-ai, Yi Tu-chan, Kang Song-san, O Hyong-chu, Chon Se-pong, Yi Myon-sang. President of the Supreme Court: Pang Hak-se. Procurate general: Chong Tong-ch'ol.

20. Politburo members who serve on the Central People's Committee are Kim Il-sung, Kim Il, Pak Song-ch'ol, Chong Chun-t'aek, Kim Man-kum, Nam Il, Ch'oe Hyon, Ho Tam, Kim Pyong-ha, Yi Chong-ok, Hong Won-kil, Hyon Mu-kwang.

21. See Nodong Sinmun, October 22, 1964.

22. See the editorial "The Historic Task of Educating the People in Communist Ideology Has Been Effectively Achieved," Kulloja, 4 (1962): 74.

23. Kim Il-sung, Report on the Work of the Central Committee to the Fourth Congress of the Workers' Party of Korea," September 11, 1961, in Selected Works, op. cit., III, 99.

24. Kim Il-sung, "On Eliminating Dogmatism and Formalism and Establishing Juche in Ideological Work," in Selected Works, op. cit., I, 591.

25. Kim Il-sung's interview with the Japanese newspaper Mainichi Shimbun, September 17, 1972.

26. Ibid.

27. See Kim Il-sung's speech "On Communist Education," delivered on November 20, 1958, in Selected Works, op. cit., II, 246-269.

28. See the editorial in Kulloja, op. cit., p. 76.

29. Ibid., p. 77.

30. See Nodong Sinmun, April 1, 1972.

31. B. C. Koh, "Ideology and Political Control in North Korea," The Journal of Politics, 32, no. 3 (August 1970): 656.

32. See the editorial in Nodong Sinmun, October 21, 1972.

3

**MASS LINE
AS A TECHNIQUE
OF LEADERSHIP**

The political development of North Korea, after its present government came to power, might be characterized as a process of building
new institutions to replace old ones, modernizing the economy to implement socialist industrialization, and transforming the traditional political culture into what Johnson has called a specifically communist "goal
culture." However, if one takes a hard look at the results of a quarter-
century's development, one is struck by the emergence of an indigenous
form of political culture, as discussed in the previous chapter, based
on Kim Il-sung's chuch'e idea. In the 1950s the Soviet models of political development were diffused in the indigenous Korean tradition and
culture, as were certain aspects of traditional Chinese culture based
on the philosophy of Confucianism, to produce North Korea's distinct
model of political culture—the Koreanization of communism.

While the Soviet model emphasizes the central role of the party's
control and the authority of its central planning, Kim's model of Korean
communism places greater emphasis on chuch'e and his personal authority to elicit the spontaneous response of the masses in the politics of
mass mobilization. Thus, ideology and organization in North Korea perform quite different functions than in the Soviet Union. Nor is the North
Korean model an exact copy of Chinese communism, since the DPRK
states officially that chuch'e was influenced by neither Mao's political
thought nor Confucian ethics, but was developed on the basis of Kim's
own revolutionary nationalism. It has been institutionalized, as discussed earlier, as a set of political symbols—beliefs, emotions or
values—for North Korea's ruling elite to justify, rationalize, and legitimize Kim's exercise of political power as well as to serve as the symbolic guide for every activity of revolution and construction. [1]

While chuch'e performs the functions of inculcating Kim's revolutionary idea of nationalism and of legitimizing his policies, his techniques of "mass line" have been effectively used to build new institutions and to mobilize the broadest possible masses of the people. "No

modern party, communist or otherwise, has ever placed so much emphasis upon the politics of modernization, " say Scalapino and Lee. [2] The
concept of the mass line is said to have originated in Kim Il-sung's
revolutionary organization in Manchuria in the 1930s. "The mass line
was the guiding principle of leadership during our revolution, " Kim
Yong-chu, Kim Il-sung's brother, explains, "to serve the masses more
faithfully, penetrating deep among them so as to educate and transform
them to become dedicated revolutionaries. It mobilized the broadest
possible masses so that they could release their latent wisdom and
energies for the cause of revolution. "[3]

After Korea's liberation from Japanese rule in 1945, Kim Il-sung
began to apply his concept of mass line as early as 1948, when he
asserted that "we must acquire the work method of explaining matters
to the masses instead of commanding them, of going deep into the
midst of the masses in order to know their feelings, teach them, and
learn from them. "[4] However, in the course of building new institutions
and of mobilizing the masses Kim has utilized two leadership techniques:
the mass line and the class line. Whenever Kim takes the mass line
approach in his leadership, he places greater emphasis on "democracy
by the people" in order to create ideological unanimity. However, when
he takes the class line approach, as he did in the 1954-59 period of
socialist revolution, he pushes for proletarian dictatorship over the
exploitative class and conducts a class struggle against such enemies
as the landlords, "compradore capitalists, " and "national traitors. "
"The historical mission of the proletarian dictatorship was, " Kim
stressed, "to wipe out the exploitative class, suppress its resistance,
and transform the working people into revolutionaries by helping them
to acquire class consciousness and then to eliminate class differences
in our country. "[5]

After 1960, however, Kim placed great emphasis on the mass line
approach. He proclaimed "the Chongsan-ni spirit and method, " the
essentials of which were that "the higher organ helps the lower; the
superior assists his inferiors and always goes down to work areas in
order to get a good grasp of actual conditions. " Thus, Kim adopted the
mass line approach, rather than the class line approach, when he
needed mass support and participation in order to execute the seven-
year economic plan by mobilizing domestic capital and resources.
Therefore, Kim continued to emphasize that

> Our best instructors are the masses and reality. All cadres
> should always learn humbly from the masses, raise their own
> level through actual work, sum up the results of their own
> work and popularize their experiences. [6]

Thus, the primary goals in the politics of mass mobilization are
to rebuild society by introducing technological revolution and to bring
about fundamental changes both in the processes of government and in

the values associated with them. This is precisely what the North Korean leadership attempted to achieve in the 1960s, when Kim Il-sung asserted, "Unless we cast away the old system, old ideas, old methods of work, and old customs of life that stand in the way of our progress, we cannot build a new, socialist society."[7] He called for the implementation of a technological, cultural, and ideological revolution in the countryside.

In the course of building a new, socialist society, the North Korean elite argued, the traditional structure of Korean society must be fundamentally altered and new institutions created or old ones restructured in order not only to absorb the sweeping changes into the society but also to generate innovation in organizational behavior. So the fundamental task of transforming the whole society of North Korea in the 1960s involved the transformation of political culture (encompassing political beliefs, styles, and the orientation of the population toward the system), on the one hand, and, on the other, the creation of new institutions by overhauling and altering the existing social and political structure. The ideological revolution and the cultural revolution were the concrete program of the North Korean leadership to transform the political culture, while the technological revolution was designed to bring about a fundamental alteration of the organizational structure of the party, government, and mass organizations in the process of coping with and responding to the social and technological changes that were sweeping throughout the society.

This chapter will focus on the efforts of the North Korean leadership to build institutions at the local level within the broader context of formulating and implementing the strategies of mass mobilization. In order to transform a political culture, total allegiance of the masses to the central instrument of change is essential. This is the main feature of any mobilization system. If a political culture is to be effective enough to sustain efficient and responsive political institutions, it must command the supreme loyalty and commitment of the population. Therefore, the primary goal of the North Korean strategies of mass mobilization, like the ones expressed in Mao Tse-tung's concept of mass line, was to transform the masses' political orientation through participation in the mass political movement. It is largely through participation in mass mobilization work that the average citizen comes to understand the true meaning of revolution and his own particular place in "the historic transformation of Korean society." Through participation comes political and revolutionary consciousness, according to Kim Il-sung, and a true revolutionary consciousness, in turn, determines correct political attitudes and sound organizational behavior.

THE STRATEGIES OF MASS MOBILIZATION

Although Kim Il-sung had begun as early as the mid-1950s to exper-
iment with the mass line approach to the solution of economic problems
(coinciding with the agrarian collectivization and the first five-year
economic plan, 1956-61), his notion of mass line was not actually fully
developed as a technique of leadership for mass mobilization until he
initiated the Chongsan-ni method in February 1960. In the 1950s, Kim
was still preoccupied with the policy of giving priority to the development of heavy industry. In this, of course, the masses of the rural
population played only a subordinate role, while the technicians and
industrial workers continued to be predominant, thus receiving the
lion's share of Kim's attention.

In February 1960, Premier Kim spent two weeks at the Chongsan-ni
collective farm in Kangso county, where he not only observed personally
the administrative methods of the management committee but also engaged directly in discussion with the members of the collective farm
about the need for mass participation in solving the problems of management and administration. The outcome of his personal observation and
direct contact with the administrative cadres at the grass-roots level
was the mass mobilization technique now commonly known as the
Chongsan-ni method. "If you want to have a thorough knowledge of
your work, you must have contact with the masses and listen to what
they say," Premier Kim asserted at the general membership meeting of
the party organization of Chongsan-ni (township). "If you talk with the
work team leaders, meet those who work well and ask their views, and
then talk with still more people by always endeavoring to hear the
voices of the masses, you will be fully informed as to who works well
and what the problems of the masses are."[8] The mass line technique
was, thus, developed as part of the mobilization strategy of the North
Korean leadership in the 1960s.

Therefore, the main themes of the mobilization strategy in the early
1960s were closely connected with the implementation of the seven-year
economic plan (1961-67). The triple themes of nationalism, socialist
revolution, and antiimperialism that characterized the ideological stance
of the North Korean regime were gradually translated into more specific
programs of "independence in politics," "self-reliance in economy,"
and "self-defense in national defense" by the mid-1960s, owing largely
to the intensification of the conflict between the Soviet Union and China
as well as to the increased military threat of the South Korean-Japanese
collusion.[9] Threatened with imminent danger from outside, the North
Korean leadership could hardly count on the support of either Communist
China or the Soviet Union. Therefore, in the course of increasing their
own accommodative capability, they devised the concept of chuch'e,
which played the key role in the mobilization system.

"Establishing chuch'e means, in a nutshell, being the master of
revolution and construction in one's own country," Kim explained.

"This means holding fast to an independent position, rejecting dependence on others, using one's own brains, believing in one's own strength, displaying the revolutionary spirit of self-reliance, and thus solving one's own problems for oneself on one's own responsibility under all circumstances. And it means adhering to the creative position of opposing dogmatism and applying the universal principles of Marxism-Leninism and the experience of other countries to suit the historical conditions and national peculiarities of one's own country."[10] Thus, the basic premise of chuch'e was in full accord with the fundamental principles of Marxism-Leninism, and the idea apparently came into being as a reflection of a new stage of the international communist movement. Chuch'e had now become an all-purpose ideology by which both international relations and the mobilization effort in domestic politics could be explained and rationalized.

The primary function of chuch'e in domestic politics, however, was to establish a close relationship between the regime and the masses by emphasizing nationalism and socialist revolution. Nationalism meant the achievement of national independence and national reunification, since "foreigners cannot carry the revolution for us."[11] Socialist revolution meant the building of a new, socialist society by restructuring the traditional social order. Both concepts required a new ideological system for the purpose of mobilizing and organizing the masses. Mobilization of the masses, of course, required winning their loyalty and commitment to the central government. In short, chuch'e had become the predominant symbol by which the North Korean leadership attempted to encourage mass participation in the political process.

Describing a proper relationship between the party and the masses, Premier Kim further stressed that "revolution and construction are the work of the masses themselves and can be accomplished successfully only when all are mobilized under the leadership of a Marxist-Leninist party. Therefore, the most important thing of all in accelerating our socialist construction and fortifying our revolutionary base is to strengthen the Party, the general staff of the revolution, and to educate and remold the people and rally them around the Party—in other words, to strengthen the ranks of revolution politically and ideologically."[12] It is, however, extremely difficult to measure the extent of mass response to such an appeal. Analysis and discussion must focus on the public statements made by the North Korean leadership about mobilization strategy in order to determine the relationship between the party and the masses.

It is now possible, on the basis of reasonably good evidence, to explain why the North Korean leadership decided in the summer of 1966 to establish chuch'e as its single ideological system. The primary goal was to mobilize and organize the masses. Following the conclusion of the Korean-Japanese normalization treaty as well as the beginning of the Cultural Revolution in China, the North Korean leadership became aware of the changes in the international environment surrounding Korea and realized that the military threat from the south was imminent, largely because the solidarity of the communist bloc had been weakened by the Sino-Soviet conflict. Under such circumstances, the only possible strategy to pursue was total mobilization of the society in order to cope with the external threat. "As the aggressive behavior of the imperialists was intensified, and revisionist ideological trends penetrated from without," Kim said, "the revisionist elements within the Party failed to implement the Party's policies sincerely, resorting to double-dealing, and they engaged in overt and covert machination to resurrect bourgeois and feudalistic Confucian ideas."[13]

However, in the process of establishing chuch'e as the central ideology of the government, party, and society at large, the North Korean leadership encountered strong opposition within the party's rank and file, and they were allegedly forced to purge this element from the party. "Our Party thoroughly exposed and smashed the insidious maneuverings of the bourgeois and revisionist elements and battled sternly against every tendency to oppose the lines and policies of the Party and undermine its unity."[14] Those who were termed "the bourgeois and revisionist elements" and purged after the ideological struggle were apparently led by Pak Kum-ch'ol, a vice chairman of the party's Central Committee as well as a member of the party's top policy-making body (the Standing Committee of the Politburo), and Li Hyo-sun, also a member of the Standing Committee of the Politburo, who was in charge of the Party's activities in relation to South Korea. They were reportedly purged following the March Plenum of the KWP in 1967.[15] Along with Pak and Li, several leading members of the party's Central Committee (all of them in charge of ideological work) were purged, including the director of propaganda and agitation (Kim To-man), the director of culture and the arts, and the director of international relations. The leading members of the central government who were purged at the same time included the vice premier in charge of arts and science (Ko Hyok), the attorney general, the minister of culture, and the director of the central news agency. Also, the chairman of the Trade Union's Central Committee and the chairman of the Socialist Youth League's Central Committee disappeared from the political scene at the same time. This was a clear indication that the establishment of chuch'e as a single ideological system created all sorts of ideological and theoretical disputes within the high echelons of the party and the government.

The issues raised in the ideological disputes over the policy of establishing chuch'e were by no means clear, but one can easily draw certain inferences on the basis of subsequent ideological developments as well as the formulation of policies. While Kim Il-sung pushed hard the policy of placing heavier emphasis on the defense buildup even at the expense of economic development, the so-called opposition group led by Pak and Li seems to have argued for a policy of moderation under the influence of the revisionist ideas originating from the Soviet Union and Eastern European countries. What the opposition group argued was precisely the revisionistic theory of economic development that emphasized balanced development in all economic sectors even if the growth rate dropped, rather than continuing to stress a higher rate of economic growth, because the pace of economic development would inevitably slow if the socialist economy reached a certain stage of development. This controversy over the theoretical problems of economic growth and development was finally resolves in March 1969, when Premier Kim decided to deal with it in a speech entitled "On Some Theoretical Problems of Socialist Economy."[16]

The gist of Kim's argument was that "the determining factor in the development of productive forces in the socialist society is certainly the higher revolutionary consciousness of the people."[17] rather than the improvement of management techniques by adopting the market mechanism or the material incentives of the capitalist system. Kim's strategy of economic development—like Mao's doctrine of military strategy, which, in the last 1960s, placed more emphasis on manpower than on weaponry—was firmly based on his concept of chuch'e, by which all the resources, both human and material, of the society were to be mobilized in order not only to build the country's defenses but also to construct the economy so as to make a quick transition to a new, socialist society. "In order to complete the socialist construction more quickly we must wholeheartedly oppose rightist opportunism in the field of economic theory," Kim expounded. "If we do not oppose the rightist tendency in economics and cultivate only selfish individualism based on pure monetary incentives, then we will not be able to arouse the people's collective heroism nor their creative consciousness, and this will in turn weaken the dictatorship of the proletariat and its political work. Thus our tasks of technological revolution and economic construction will never be successfully achieved."[18] Kim's main purpose in writing this speech was to attack the elements within the party and government who were under the influence of so-called revisionism and had also committed rightist errors by accepting the capitalistic method of economic management by providing material incentives.

The theoretical controversy over the rate and speed of economic growth and development as well as over the party's policy line that took place in the 1966-67 period somewhat resembled the policy disputes and subsequent purges of August 1956, when the leading members of both the Soviet and Yenan factions, led by Pak Ch'ang-ok and Ch'oe Ch'ang-ik, respectively, were purged from the policy-making machinery of the KWP.[19] However, in comparing the 1956 disputes with those of 1966, one is struck by the important function of ideology in the latter controversy, when the North Korean leadership declared itself to have developed the policy of "independence in politics," "self-reliance in economy,' and "self-defense in national defense."[20] Following the Conference of the Party's Representatives in October 1966, North Korea began to assert the concept of chuch'e as the single ideological system and as the thought of Kim Il-sung. Kim was elevated to a theoretical position equal to that of Lenin and Mao. He has been called not only "the great leader of the revolution and the genius in the theory of Marxism-Leninism" but also "the greatest patriot and national hero" and "the exceptional leader of the international communist movement and also of the labor movement of the world."[21]

Four years later, at the Fifth Congress of the KWP on November 3, 1970, Kim concluded succinctly that "today the unitary ideological system has been solidly established within our Party and the whole Party has attained monolithic unity and cohesion based on Marxist-Leninist ideas, the chuch'e ideas of our Party." Thus, "the establishment of chuch'e in ideology is a great victory in the realm of the ideological revolution that has freed our people from the shackles of obsolete ideas detrimental to their consciousness of national independence."[22]

LOCAL GOVERNMENT AS AN INSTRUMENT OF MASS MOBILIZATION

The primary goal of the North Korean leadership in the 1960s, as mentioned earlier, was to reorient the population toward new values compatible with social change and political modernization. To achieve such a lofty goal, the North Korean elite formulated a variety of developmental strategies in which the problems of participation, identity, and legitimacy became the main focus of attack in the mid-1960s. In order to attract the masses to participate in numerous developmental projects while at the same time making them closely identified with and committed to the regime, the North Korean leadership paid special attention to the development of local administrative systems. The local administrative cadres served as a transmission belt through which the programs and policies of the party and the central government were to be disseminated and through which the grass-roots opinions and attitudes of the local population toward the central government were channeled back to the central leadership. "The people's committees at all levels," Premier Kim emphasized, "are the most comprehensive transmission belt linking the Party with the popular masses, the executor of the lines and policies of our Party, and the householder in charge of the people's living." Therefore, a thorough knowledge of "the administrative system" at the local level is essential to our understanding and evaluation of developmental projects in North Korea.[23]

After the completion of collectivization, the North Korean leadership proceeded with the administration and management of collective farms with two important goals in mind: a rapid increase in agrarian production to pay for the industrailization projects under the first five-year plan (1956-61), and the transformation of the rural villages into a new, socialist society. In order to achieve such goals, it was necessary to set up an administrative and management network to provide an effective planning and control system for industry and agriculture.[24]

as well as to increase ideological indoctrination and education, aimed at generating revolutionary consciousness on the part of the peasant population and encouraging their participation in developmental projects. Since the administrative processes of rural development in North Korea were, in many respects, similar to what the Chinese leadership attempted in order to solve the developmental problems of rural society, it would be interesting to analyze the political and administrative capacity of the North Korean leadership in the light of Mao's concept of the mass line approach, his educational methods, and his organizational techniques of mass persuasion and participation.

Immediately following the completion of collectivization, the North Korean leadership adopted a policy of merging the collective farms into larger units at the basic level. Within the lowest administrative unit, the li (similar to a township and consisting of a number of villages), the collective farms were amalgamated to form the basic production unit. The reason for this policy, as explained by the regime, was to close the wide gap between the industrial sector and the rural society by introducing ideological, technological, and cultural revolution under a new and effective administrative system.[25] There were, after the amalgamation of the collective farms, more than a quarter of a million administrative cadres working in the administrative system of North Korea.

The term "administative cadres" here refers to those who are engaged in a variety of administrative functions in the party, in governmental bureaucracy, and in judicial and educational work throughout the country.[26] This group of people is under constant pressure from the central leadership to establish and maintain a close link with the masses while at the same time keeping their own class line. "Only when the functionaries go among the masses and penetrate the realities of their lives can they grasp thoroughly their creative opinions and demands and correctly comprehend and scientifically analyze and assess the changes taking place in those realities, and take appropriate measures in good time," Premier Kim instructed his administrative cadres. However, Kim also called for "principles and concrete ways for correctly combining the class line with the mass line and dictatorship with democracy in state activity in order to strengthen the dictatorship of the proletariat and enhance its function and role."[27]

Thus, the class line here meant the administrative cadres' political loyalty based on the ideology of chuch'e, while the mass line meant the administrative competence of the cadres to get the masses of people to participate in the implementation of a variety of policies. The local administrators were expected not only to understand the correct policy line sent down from the party's policy-making center but also to come to grips with the opinions and attitudes of the masses so that they could mobilize them effectively and organize them to participate in the process of policy implementation. This has been a common problem for the administrators in both North Korea and Communist China: the establishment of a link between the "red" demand for political loyalty and the "expert" demand for technical competence.

In the process of recruiting the administrative cadres at the grass-roots level, the North Korean leadership placed strong emphasis on class line: recruitment on the basis of class background and loyalty to the regime rather than on the basis of educational background or professional competence. In the formative stage of the regime, the North Korean leadership, in operating the government machinery and running the economy, relied heavily on the intellectuals who had acquired professional and technical training during the Japanese colonial rule. "They, as intellectuals of a colony, had been subjected to national oppression and discrimination by foreign imperialism and, therefore, had a national and democratic revolutionary spirit," Kim Il-sung admitted. Therefore, "our Party took into account their revo-lutionary spirit and adopted the line of actively drawing them into the building of a new society and thus remolding them into intellectuals serving the working people."[28] Many of them were, thus, reeducated or remolded by the new ideology to become "socialist intellectuals"; others were replaced by the so-called "new intellectuals of working class origin." The new generation of administrative cadres was con-sidered to possess assured political loyalty and sound class origin, although they were relatively weak in professional training and techni-cal competence.

The basic dilemma in operating the administrative system was how to bridge the gap between the lofty goals of quick industrialization and economic development, whose achievement requires a large number of professionally competent administrators, and the practical problems of training the newly recruited cadres who were politically loyal to the regime but professionally less competent. In order to solve this prob-lem, the North Korean leadership attached a great deal of importance to the orientation and education of rural cadres. Cadre training was, thus, directed to create an "independent work capability," which meant that a local administrative unit should be able to implement policies without intervention from the county or provincial cadres. It meant that the leader at the li level should be able to use mass line techniques: getting work done by mass persuasion rather than coercion, and implementing policies by directly participating in the work rather than issuing administrative commands.

Although considerable effort had been made to train local cadres in administrative skills, the new cadres were unable to cope with the quickly expanding industry and collective farm. Therefore, the training programs of the basic administrative cadres were stepped up greatly following the development of the Chongsan-ni method by the direct participation of Premier Kim.

Since the mass line techniques developed by the North Korean leadership were fully conceptualized and put into operation in the form of the Congsan-ni method and the Taean work system, an analysis of

58

their organizational methods might serve as an active illustration of the mass line approach to developmental problems. It may also provide a picture of how the mass line techniques were implemented at the local level of the administrative system.

A description of the Chongsan-ni collective farm is interesting because it served as the model collective whose administrative system other collectives were instructed to emulate. Of average size, it consisted of 650 farm households with a total population of 3400, of whom 1200 were accounted full members of the collective. The rest included the children, the elderly, and the disabled. This farm maintained 2300 hectares (ha) of land, which may be broken down as follows: rice field, 660 ha; dry field, 260 ha; orchard, 210 ha; mulberry tree farm, 20 ha. This farm also bred 300 hogs, 500 rabbits, 1000 chickens, and 300 cows and oxen. The members of the collective were divided into 20 workteams, and a total of 104 tractors were employed in farming. Seven trucks were used for transportation.

This farm operated a technical high school that specialized in forestry and a nine-grade middle school for the members' children. It also maintained 11 nursery schools and 14 day care centers. The professional people on the farm included 84 technicians and mechanics, 200 drivers, and 10 physicians. Each household operated a sewing machine and a television set. Thus, this collective farm was by no means an average collective in material or cultural standards, but was above average in its income and the material well-being of its people. However, the North Korean leadership insisted that it was a typical collective farm.

The management committee of this collective farm performed each and every administrative function of local government. After the amalgamation of the collectives into the li administrative units, the management committee took over many of the administrative functions of the li people's committee, which in the past was the basic administrative unit, and became the sole administrative agency of agricultural production, distribution, consumption, and exchange in the village. In order to provide smooth administrative reorganization, the chairman of the li people's committee was concurrently appointed to serve as the chairman of the management committee of the collective farm at the basic administrative level. One of the important functions of the chairman, according to Kim Il-sung, was that "he should have regard for the opinions of his subordinates and kindly lead them in their work, and those below, for their part, should give him help and advice so that he may thoroughly acquaint himself with his job."[29]

One of the administrative problems described by Premier Kim was that of coordination between the party committee and the management committee. "The Party is not a party of the Party Committee chairman, but of all Party members. The Party members should all work actively for proper management of the cooperative and bear the responsibility for the work of the cooperative whether it goes well or not," Kim declared. "The Chinese ideograph for 'party' symbolizes 'group.'

That is, the party is an organization not of one man but of a multitude of party members who fight in a group. The management of the cooperative should be guided through the medium of the Party organization."[30] Therefore, Kim called on the party to exercise its leadership and control over the management committee of the collective farm.

Another basic problem of administrative management at the basic level with which Kim was concerned was the question of how the collective leadership system was to be established and maintained at the production unit. In two important speeches, "For the Correct Management of the Socialist Rural Economy" and "On Further Developing the Taean Work System," he stressed the most ideal and rational form of administrative system that should be instituted by a collective management system. "The county people's committee and the management board should discuss work norms seriously and draw up a table of standard norms," Kim asserted. "This should not be decided by any one person at the desk. It should be discussed at a general membership meeting of all cooperative members."[31] What emerges out of these two speeches is the fundamental problem of establishing a close link between the bureaucrats and the masses. Thus, what the North Korean leadership needed at this juncture were the Chinese methods of mass line and hsia-fang (going down) in order to have the masses participate in the implementation of party policies.

The Taean work system, originating in the Taean electric machine factory in November 1962, was a good example of how the North Korean leadership attempted to introduce the concept of collective leadership in the industrial management system. In the early 1960s the North Korean elite began to replace the one-man management system, patterned on Soviet industrial management, with a collective management system in which the party's committee chairman participated in the policy making along with the plant manager. Under this collective management system the plant manager was directly responsible to the party committee of the plant in receiving and implementing the party's policies, but the chairman of the party's committee was to take full responsibility in handling political problems such as intervention from higher officials and the participation of the plant manager in political affairs.

The rationale for this new system was, basically, to broaden the base of mass support by eliminating bureaucratic red tape and by drawing the working masses to participate in the management and administration of party policy at the basic administrative level. By instituting the collective management system, the North Korean leadership expected to generate more energy and power among the working masses and transform them into a dynamic force by which the industrialization programs could be achieved. At the same time, political and moral appeals to the masses were stepped up, but there was no capital investment or material incentive for the workers to produce more. Thus, instead of the individual worker receiving the bonus earned by his own hard work, the extra earnings were placed in the trust fund of a plant and more than half the money was spent to improve the welfare and the cultural and athletic programs of the industrial workers so as to benefit everyone rather than an individual worker.

While the old system of industrial management is said to have "retained capitalist elements" and "elements of bureaucracy, departmentalism and individualism," the new system incorporated "the principle of collective, communist life."[32] Therefore, "the Taean work system is radically different from the old one," Premier Kim asserted. "In this system superiors help their subordinates, the well-informed are teaching the less-informed, all the people are helping each other as comrades, and all the workshops are cooperating closely."[33] In the old system, "the Party functionaries and the administrators were not on good terms with each other," a fact that hampered the coordination of the party and the management committees at the local level. However, under the new system of collective management, "the Party committee manages and operates the factory as its supreme leading organ, and all the Party members, workers, and technicians participate in its management," Kim stressed. [34]

The Taean work system was, in many respects, a direct transfer of the Chongsan-ni method from rural economic management to the management of industrial plants. The characteristics of these two methods were also concrete examples of mass line techniques in action. One of the most striking solutions to the problems of bureaucracy and administrative tardiness at the local level was the shaking up of the basic-level organization by introducing mass line techniques and the collective management system. This was done on the basis of the political and moral appeals of chuch'e rather than by introducing a material incentive system. These efforts were somewhat similar to what the Chinese leadership attempted to achieve during the socialist education campaign just before the launching of the Great Proletarian Cultural Revolution in 1965. Thus, the strategies of mass mobilization in the 1960s in North Korea and Communist China seem to have been parallel, though the North Korean strategy was firmly based on Kim's concept of chuch'e while the Chinese strategy was derived from the thought of Mao Tse-tung.

In this chapter I have focused on some of the reasons why chuch'e had to be evolved into a monolithic ideological system within the broad context of the politics of mass mobilization. I have also analyzed the institutional matrix of the local level administrative units and their role in the implementation of the party's policies. What is most striking about the administrative process in North Korea is the strong emphasis on the role of a single ideology in creating new values in the society, a common characteristic of developing societies, as well as on the role of mass line techniques, which are basically prerequisites for the establishment of a close link between the central instrument of change and the masses. These are perhaps inevitable techniques of organization in developing societies, by means of which a certain stage of development can be achieved.

North Korea is by no means a mature industrial society, though its leadership claims that it has reached a socialist stage of development, nor is it a totalitarian society in the full sense described by Carl Friedrich and Zbigniew Brzezinski in Totalitarian Dictatorship and Autocracy. It is still a developing society striving hard to achieve the primary goal of industrialization; yet it is, in many respects, quite different from the other developing societies of Asia and Africa because it maintains a highly developed mobilization and a tight organizational control over its population. Therefore, North Korea might still be characterized as a mobilization type of society, one of the stages a developing nation has to go through in the process of modernization.

Administrative systems play an important role in measuring political modernization, because bureaucracy, according to Max Weber, is a manifestation par excellence of modernity. Bureaucracy is also an instrument and expression of rationality, increasing complexity, and technological development, and, therefore, it tends to function in a modern society as a neutral tool of the ruling elite. However, the North Korean bureaucracy is perhaps one of the most politicized in the modern world, as mentioned earlier. There has been tension between competence and loyalty as industrialization has advanced and the bureaucratic organization has expanded. The North Korean leadership has solved such problems by introducing mass line techniques and collective management and shaking up the bureaucratic organization at the local level. Bureaucracy as an institution has its own internal dynamics; therefore, political intervention may not resolve organizational problems. Thus, it remains to be seen whether or not the North Korean bureaucracy will ultimately emerge, when North Korean society achieves modernization, as a dynamic political force or will continue to function as an instrument of change.

NOTES

1. See Sung Chul Yang, "Ideology in South and North Korean Politics: A Comparative Analysis," paper delivered at the Twenty-Sixth Annual Meeting of the Association for Asian Studies in Boston, April 1-3, 1974. Also see the interesting argument in Bruce G. Cumings, "Kim's Korean Communism," Problems of Communism, 23, no. 2 (March-April 1974): 27-40.

2. See Robert A. Scalapino and Chong-sik Lee, Communism in Korea, (Berkely: University of California Press, 1972), V p. 375.

3. Kim Yong-chu, "The Respected Leader Kim Il-sung Is the Great Man of Thought and the Great Theorist in Our Times," Nodong Sinmun, (The Workers Daily) April 13, 1972.

4. See Kim Il-sung's report to the Second Congress of the North Korean Workers Party, March 28, 1948, in Kim Il-sung Sonjip (The

Selected Works of Kim Il-sung) (Pyongyang: The Korean Workers Press, 1960), I, 111.

5. Kim Il-sung, Selected Works, op. cit., V, 115.

6. Kim Il-sung's report to the Fourth Party Congress, September 11, 1961, in ibid., III, 57-204.

7. Kim Il-sung, For the Correct Management of the Socialist Rural Economy, (Pyongyang: Foreign Languages Publishing House, 1969), p. 43.

8. Ibid., p. 27.

9. Kim Il-sung, "The Present Situation and the Task Confronting Our Party," report to the Conference of the Workers' Party of Korea, October 5, 1966, Collected Works, op. cit. IV, p. 100-187.

10. Kim Il-sung, "On Immediate Political and Economic Policies of the Democratic People's Republic of Korea and Some International Problems," answers to questions raised by newsmen of the Japanese daily Yomiuri Shimbun, January 15, 1972.

11. "The Great Leader Comrade Kim Il-sung Is the Founder and Leader of the First State of Proletarian Dictatorship in Our Country," Minchu Choson (Democratic Korea), January 10, 1972.

12. Kim Il-sung, "Report on the Work of the Central Committee to the Fifth Congress of the Workers' Party of Korea." The full text is in The Pyongyang Times, November 3, 1970. See pt. V, "For the Strengthening of Party Work," p. 21.

13. Ibid., p. 22.

14. See Hayashi Takehiko, Kta Chosen to Minami Chosen (North Korea and South Korea) (Tokyo: Saimaru Publishing Society, 1971), p. 151.

15. Kim Il-sung, "On Some Theoretical Problems of Socialist Economy," Nodong Sinmun, March 1, 1969.

16. Ibid., p. 3.

17. Ibid.

18. For a discussion of this purge, see Kim Ch'ang-sun, Pukhan Sip-o-nyon Sa (Fifteen-Year History of North Korea) (Seoul: Chimun kak, 1961).

19. See the editorial "Let Us Defend Our Independence!," Nodong Sinmun, August 12, 1966.

20. For typical praise in the personality cult of Kim Il-sung, see Pak Song-ch'ol's speech on the second day of the Fifth Congress of the KWP, November 4, 1970, Nodong Sinmun, October 5, 1970.

21. Kim Il-sung's report to the Fifth Party Congress, op. cit., pt. V.

22. For an interesting definition of "the administrative system," see Fred W. Riggs, ed., Frontiers of Development Administration (Durham, N. C.: Duke University Press, 1970).

23. For an excellent description of the control mechanism in the North Korean countryside, see Chong-sik Lee and Nam Sik Kim, "Control and Administrative Mechanisms in the North Korean Countryside," The Journal of Asian Studies, 29, no. 2 (February 1970).

24. As a result of this policy, the total number of collective farms was reduced from 16, 032 to 3, 843. See Chong-sik Lee, "The Socialist Revolution in the North Korean Countryside, " Asian Survey, 2, no. 8 (October 1962): 11.

25. See, for example, "A Study of Personnel Administration in North Korea, " in Yongu Nonch'ong (Research Forum) (Seoul: Institute for Far Eastern Affairs), March 1971. This article concluded that there were about 320, 000 in the government bureaucracy as of 1963. See p. 19.

26. This quotation is from an article entitled "The Great Leader Comrade Kim Il-sung Is the Founder and Leader of the First State of Proletarian Dictatorship in Our Country, " Minchu Chosen (Democratic Korea) , January 9, 1972.

27. "The Report of the KWP Conference," Collected Works, IV p. 162.

28. Kim Il-sung, Rural Economy, op. cit., p. 30.

29. Ibid., p. 9.

30. Ibid., p. 17.

31. Kim Il-sung, "On Further Developing the Taean Work System, " speech delivered at the Enlarged Meeting of the Party Committee of the Taean Electric Machine Factory, November 9, 1962. (Pyongyang: Foreign Languages Publishing House, 1968), p. 2.

32. Ibid., p. 3.

33. Ibid., p. 6.

34. For a perceptive analysis of North Korea's management system, see Daniel S. Juhn, "A Comparative Study of the North Korean Managerial System at the Factory Level, " Journal of Korean Affairs, 2, no. 1 (April 1972): 16-21.

4

POLICY DISPUTES
OVER THE STRATEGY
OF DEVELOPMENT

The death of Stalin and the subsequent de-Stalinization movement created severe repercussions within the KWP. The response in Korea was not so sharp as the Polish or Hungarian uprisings, but some sort of crisis took place within the Korean party. According to the North Korean publications, Kim Il-sung, chairman of the party's Central Committee, was directly challenged, and when he later purged this antiparty group he referred to this internal struggle as the crisis of August 1956. [1]

After the death of Stalin, while Malenkov's New Course was being followed in the East European countries, North Korea was moving toward a more tightened economic system by launching its three-year economic plan for postwar reconstruction and development. By the time of the Third Party Congress in April 1956, North Korea officially claimed that it was entering the stage of the "socialist revolution." Upon the completion of the three-year plan in 1956, North Korea announced its first five-year plan, to extend from 1957 to 1961; its objective—to build the foundations for socialism and the development of heavy industry—continued to be stressed.

North Korea followed closely the later Khrushchev formula that was to stress a return to an economic policy of maintaining heavy capital development while at the same time striving to improve agricultural productivity and revitalize the economy. In reviewing the economic achievement of the first five-year plan at the Fourth Party Congress in September 1961, Kim asserted: "During the period of the five-year plan the main task of socialist construction was to industrialize and provide the basic needs of our people. In order to carry out this task successfully our Party took the basic policy of giving priority to heavy industry and simultaneous development of agriculture and light industry. [2]

As for the theoretical justification, Kim Il-sung condemned the antiparty faction's opposition to his economic policy in terms similar to those used by Khrushchev, who warned that abandoning the priority on heavy industry is "nothing but slandering our Party. . . . a belching of the rightist deviation, a regurgitation of views hostile to Leninism. "[3]

An indication that the Korean infraparty struggle was crucial was an urgent visit in the summer of 1956 by Anastas I. Mikoyan and Peng Teh-huai (the former commander of the Chinese volunteers in the Korean War) to North Korea in an attempt to mediate between the two rival groups. By the end of the Korean War, the nucleus of the national or indigenous communists was purged from the North Korean party leadership, but two powerful factions emerged—the so-called Russian-returned "Muscovites" and the Chinese-returned "Yenan faction"—within the Party.

After the Third Congress in April 1956, Kim Il-sung took a long trip to the Soviet Union and the East European countries. His purpose was to extend North Korea's gratitude for the economic aid rendered by the fraternal countries during the postwar economic construction and to solicit further economic assistance in order to carry out the first five-year plan successfully. During his absence of two months, two prominent party theoreticians among Kim's lieutenants revealed their sentiments against the personality cult in North Korea by publishing articles in the party's journals. Both authors, Cabinet Member Pak Ch'ang-ok and Vice Premier Ch'oe Ch'ang-ik, were known to be in the inner circle of the fifteen-member Politburo of the party. Pak came to North Korea from the Soviet Union and became known as one of the leading theoreticians of the Russian-returned group. He was once the editor of Nodong Sinmun and later was promoted to the standing committee of the Politburo. Following the reorganization of the party in August 1953, Pak became one of the three vice chairmen of the party's Central Committee. The three vice chairmen took over the functions of the secretariat of the party, which was abolished at the Sixth Plenum. Some circles interpreted this promotion as a reward to Pak Ch'ang-ok for his contribution in carrying out the purge of the clique of Pak Hon-yong, the vice premier and foreign minister, in the spring of that year. [4] However, in 1954 Pak was transfered to the posts of vice premier and chairman of the State Control Commission, and the party announced that he had resigned from the vice chairmanship of the Central Committee. No reason was given.

Ch'oe Ch'ang-ik, one of the Chinese-returned theoreticians who came to North Korea with the Yenan group, is the author of the chapters on the history of the Korean Communist Party in Choson Minjok Haebang T'uchang-sa (History of the Korean People's Struggle for Liberation), a product of writers at Kim Il-sung University, published in Pyongyang in 1949. [5] In 1953, following the Sixth Plenum, Ch'oe was elevated to the Politburo of the Central Committee and was given the cabinet post of finance minister.

Ch'oe and Pak praised the process of de-Stalinization in the Soviet Union in the course of denouncing Kim Il-sung and pointing out that the cult of personality had been excessive in North Korea. They urged that North Korea pursue the course of the Soviet Union, denouncing the one-man dictatorship and doing away with the personality cult. It was clear that they were attempting to oust Kim Il-sung by identifying him as a little Stalin in North Korea. [6]

In August, on his return to North Korea, Kim reported to the Sixth Plenum of the Central Committee on his trip. At this plenum, one of the leaders of the Yenan group, Yun Kong-hum, deputy minister of light industry, led the attack on Kim Il-sung, the main charges being that Kim was too dictatorial, his policy was "antipeople," and he did not pay sufficient wages to the workers. Especially in the field of economic policy, he was denounced for his inattention to agriculture and for giving priority to heavy industry. Ch'oe and Pak approved Yun's attack during the discussion session following the reports and speeches. Disputes over the policy of economic development continued until the December Plenum of the Central Committee, when the party adopted the basic policy line.

Despite these criticisms, Kim Il-sung had enough supporters within the Central Committee to defeat his opponents at the plenum. While the debates raged, Ch'oe and Yun made an attempt to escape to Communist China, fearing the consequences of their attack on the party leadership. However, they were caught by the security police and subsequently purged from the party with seven other collaborators in the party's Central Committee. Immediately following Kim's triumph over his rivals, the party intensified its propaganda compaign against the anti-Kim group, who were denounced as antiparty factionalists at the First Party Conference on March 3-6, 1958. The severity of the struggle within the party was indicated by purges lasting from 1956 to the convening of the Fourth Party Congress on September 11-18, 1961. This purge was reflected in the composition of the Central Committee elected by the Fourth Congress. Forty-three out of seventy of the regular members and 32 out of 44 of the alternate members were dropped from the Central Committee, making a total of 75 members were removed from the 114-member Central Committee of the KWP. At the Fourth Congress, 96 new members were added to the 135-member Central Committee of the party, thereby changing its structure considerably.

Kim Tu-bong, leader of the Yenan group and first chairman of the North Korean Workers' Party at the time of union with the New People's Party and the North Korean Communist Party in August 1946, was alleged to be associated in this dissension but was not arrested until the end of 1958. The leaders of the anti-Kim group were mostly from Communist China except for Pak and one other Russian returnee. There was a rumor that the Russian returned leaders were directly influenced by the supporters of Khrushchev in the Soviet Union, who dislike the North Korean policy, but there was no evidence to verify this. It is possible that the two "Muscovites" were discontented mainly with Kim's domestic policy and allied themselves with the Yenan faction to oust him.

The Yenan faction was closely related to Communist China in ideology and experience. This group might have been dissatisfied with Kim's domestic policy because of its dependence on Soviet direction and his unresponsiveness to suggestions from those who had had some experience in Communist China. To Kim Il-sung, these antiparty people were "right deviationists." Nodong Sinmun , the organ of the Party's Central Committee, noted that ". . . the anti-party group opposed the Party's correct policy to give priority to heavy industry in the first five year plan . . . these doctrinaires were walking backward and could not see the reality and believed it was impossible for us to carry out the economic plan."[7]

The policy dispute between Kim Il-sung, who survived the challenge, and the opposition group, who were later labeled "antiparty factionalists," focused on the pace of the industrialization programs, the collectivization of agriculture, and the North Korean approach to the Soviet policy of de-Stalinization. The opposition was apparently led by Pak Ch'ang-ok, a Soviet Korean who wielded enormous power as vice premier and chairman of the State Planning Commission in the postwar period (1954-56). From the charges that the KWP directed at the so-called "antiparty factionalists," one can surmise that the policy positions taken by Pak and his followers were influenced by Khrushchev's new policy line. They seem to have argued that the North Korean regime must pay more attention to the workers and the peasants, since they have been squeezed enough in bringing about the successful achievement of postwar economic development. The established target for the first five-year plan was, from their viewpoint, too unrealistic; the population could hardly be asked to sacrifice for five more years in addition to what it had already suffered. Especially in view of what was taking place in the Soviet Union and in the other countries of Eastern Europe, the opposition contended that the question of whether a policy of emphasizing the development of heavy industry at the expense of consumer goods should be resolved.

The attempt by the Khrushchev leadership to change the course of economic development in North Korea was revealed later, when the North Korean leadership supported the Chinese positions in the height of the Sino-Soviet conflicts and Soviet-North Korean relations reached their lowest ebb. Nodong Sinmun, under the title "Let Us Strictly Observe the Rules of Mutual Relations Between the Fraternal Parties and Fraternal States," attacked Soviet interference in North Korea's domestic affairs when it asserted that "some comrades did not understand our Party's policy of socialist construction in the past period. They [meaning the Soviet critics] criticized our policies without any knowledge of our situation that our Five Year Economic Plan was nothing but an illusion; we should not construct the machine building industry; the speed of our agricultural collectivization was too fast; and how could we collectivize our agricultural management without the farm machinery, etc."[8]

To continue the policy of giving priority ot the development of heavy industry, of course, required continued capital and technical assistance from the Soviet Union and the East European countries, as well as the support of the North Korean population in maintaining a frugal standard of living and extended working hours for five more years. The workers and the peasant population, the opposition reasoned, needed better living conditions and more consumer goods rather than a demand for greater sacrifice and harder work.

The controversy over whether the development of heavy industry was to be given priority over the development of light and consumer industry seems to have persisted from late 1955 to late 1956. However, the retreat of the opposition group was clearly evidenced by the fact that Pak Ch'ang-ok, under attack by Kim Il-sung as early as December 1955, was removed from the chairmanship of the State Planning Commission in January 1956. When the antiparty factionalists were finally defeated and ousted from the Central Committee of the KWP, they were charged with being "revisionists," meaning that they were closely associated with the policies of the Soviets.

Because the policy issues were still being challenged within the leadership structure of the KWP, Kim Il-sung and his followers were quite undecided on the question of whether or not the first five-year plan was to be unveiled at the Third Party Congress of the KWP, which convened in April 1956. The omission of a formal presentation or explanation of the five-year plan at the Congress was another indication that the conflict over industrialization and collectivization of agriculture was far from being settled.

Apparently, a compromise solution was reached temporarily, since opponents as well as proponents of a new economic policy recognized that the success of the five-year plan would depend largely on the willingness of the Soviet Union and the East European countries to provide the necessary capital funds. At any rate, the official delegation headed by Premier Kim Il-sung made a seven-week tour (June-July 1956) to the Soviet Union and the East European countries to solicit the capital funds to launch the five-year plan. Though upon its return the delegation reported to a mass rally that the Soviet Union had promised a large sum of economic aid to finance the five-year plan, the exact figure was not disclosed at the meeting.[9] The policy of implementation of the first five-year plan (1957-61) was, thus, not formally adopted until the First Conference of the Party's Representatives was convened two years later, in March 1958.

A decisive factor that influenced the policy shift, at the end of 1956, from "learn from the Soviet Union" to self-reliance was the failure of the North Korean delegation to obtain the expected amount of aid from the Soviet Union and the East European countries to finance the five-year plan. The alternatives now left to the North Korean leadership were to carry through the original five-year plan or to modify it. The latter alternative apparently was the Soviet desire, supported vehemently by the opposition group in the KWP. The North Korean leadership subsequently acknowledged Soviet interference in the formulation of North Korea's five-year plan when an editorial in Nodong Sinmun charged that they (the Soviet leaders) "challenged us, saying that our five-year plan was an illusion, that we don't need to construct a machine-building industry, and that the speed of our agricultural collectivization was too fast, although they were not familiar with the realities of our country."[10] The persistent policy conflict between

Kim Il-sung and the so-called "antiparty group" in 1956 culminated in the final adoption of the policy of self-reliance at the December (1956) Plenum of the KWP's Central Committee.

After failing to acquire a substantial amount of aid from the Soviet bloc countries in order to finance the first five-year plan, the North Korean leadership began to develop new strategies of economic development based on the Maoist policy of self-reliance, which was actually designed to mobilize the domestic resources, both economic and human, to meet the requirements of economic development.[11] This process of shifting from a policy of foreign dependency to one of self-reliance was accompanied not only by a series of continuous policy debates but also by a systematic elimination of opposition leaders within the leadership structure of the KWP.[12] The policy shift was also greatly stimulated by the changes taking place in Soviet policy toward its bloc countries in general and, more specifically, by the new concept of "different roads to socialism" promoted by the Khrushchev leadership in the Soviet Union after the 20th Congress of the CPSU.[13]

The process of adopting a new policy of self-reliance, of course, required psychological preparation as well as ideological indoctrination between 1957 and 1958. To prepare psychologically for a new policy line, the North Korean leadership had already begun to promulgate the concept of chuch'e (self-identity). Kim Il-sung had already delivered a speech on the establishment of national identity in December 1955, the purpose of which was to call on the party's propaganda workers to initiate a "rectification" campaign.[14] The editorials of Nodong Sinmun, an official organ of the Central Committee of the KWP, began to promote the policy of self-reliance based on chuch'e in 1956. The essence of chuch'e, according to an editorial, "For a Correct Understanding of Chuch'e," is the model on which "Comrade Kim Il-sung is able to apply creatively the general theory of Marxism-Leninism to the concrete realities of Korea." Therefore, chuch'e was to function as an ideology by which "the international obligations and national goals were to be integrated" in external affairs and by which "the leadership and the masses were to be closely linked" on the domestic front.[15] The concept is certainly not chauvinism, the editorial insisted, but a criterion by which to judge whether or not the general theory of Marxism-Leninism is being mechanically or creatively applied to the specific conditions of Korea.

It took almost a whole year to prepare both the party cadres and the population psychologically and ideologically to accept a new policy line based on the concept of chuch'e. A careful analysis of the editorial comments of Nodong Sinmun throughout 1956 shed some interesting light on the subject. They asserted that the regime was beginning to lay the groundwork for the policy shift from dependency on the Soviet bloc, in which the major slogan was "Learn from the Soviet Experience," to self-reliance, in which the major emphasis was to be placed on the revolutionary tradition of guerrilla warfare in Manchuria.[16]

What are, then the essential components of the policy of self-reliance? To achieve the economic goals established in the first five-year plan, the North Korean leadership could no longer count on the support of the Soviet bloc countries; thus, they were forced to adopt a policy to mobilize the domestic resources and human energy of their own people, just as the Chinese Communists had done during the period of the revolutionary movement. The Chinese leadership developed a revolutionary strategy during the Kiangsi and Yenan periods based on Mao's concept of mass line, which carried the Chinese Communists to final victory in 1949. When the Chinese leaders shifted their own "Learn from the Soviet Union" policy to one of self-reliance in 1956, they adopted their own revolutionary model to solve the problems of economic growth and development without outside support. [17] This was precisely what the North Korean leadership attempted to do in formulating development strategies in the first five-year plan period. Thus, Kim Il-sung began to glorify his own revolutionary experience in the war against Japan and to circulate stories of revolutionary heroes in order to inculcate the spirit of self-reliance in the population at large. Of course, it was not an easy task to shift from the policy of "Learn from the Soviet Union," since the elite and the population of North Korea had been taught for almost a dozen years to think of the Soviet Union as their liberator and the model of development. To justify his own position and educate the population as to the need for a policy change, Kim Il-sung seems to have accepted the Chinese model as his method of applying the general theory of Marxism-Leninism to the actual conditions of North Korea. Thus, Kim claimed that the real contribution of the Chinese Communists to Marxism and Leninism "is the creative application of Marxism-Leninism to the specific conditions of China, which the people in North Korea must not only admire and praise but also learn," in order to build socialism in North Korea. [18]

Recalling the Chinese experience with the revolutionary movement, and the emergence of the thought of Mao Tse-tung as the doctrine of the Chinese revolutionary movement in the early 1950s, Kim Il-sung stepped up his campaign to propagandize the revolutionary experience of the Korean partisan group in Manchuria in the 1930s and began to circulate widely his November 1958 speech "On the Education of Communism." This speech, like Liu Shao-ch'i's two important speeches, "How to Be a Good Communist" (1934) and "On the Party's Mass Line" (1945), called on the party's propaganda workers to cultivate and reform themselves, among other things, so as to carry out "uninterrupted revolution" in North Korea and establish a work based on the mass line approach. [19] In the process of implementing the policy based on mass line, the party workers were called on "not only to study and cultivate themselves but also to form a close link with the masses, and work among them." "In order to establish a close link with the masses," Kim asserted, "you must work with the masses and breathe with the masses." [20] This is precisely what Mao said about the concept of mass line—from the masses to the masses.

The essence of mass line as expounded by the North Korean leadership, like the Chinese concept, was to "trust the creativity and the wisdom of the masses" first, and then go in among them "in order to find out their interests and aspirations." What the party workers found out about the masses should be reflected in the party's policy implementation—if the party work was to be successful. Therefore, the quality of the leadership method was to be evaluated on the basis of whether or not the policy was implemented throught the mass line approach. In view of what was taking place in the Soviet bloc countries, the North Korean leadership seems to have assessed correctly the political trend as well as the interest and aspiration of the North Korean people since they, like the Hungarian and Polish people, aspired to "independence" and "nationalism" following the 20th Congress of the CPSU. After more than a decade of dependency on the Soviet Union, the North Korean population naturally sought national independence more than anything else.

The mass line approach based on the spirit of national identity or nationalism, like the Chinese concept of mass line during the 1957-51 period, was successful in mobilizing the energy of the native population and the domestic resources to fulfill the goal set in the first five-year plan. [21] It was quite apparent that the policy shift from Soviet dependency to self-reliance was made at the December (1956) Plenum of the KWP and that the new policy of self-reliance was fully implemented beginning in 1957, when Kim Il-sung asserted that "the economic plan for 1957 can be achieved only by mobilizing all our domestic resources and human energy." [22] Immediately following the adoption of this new policy, the KWP called on its rank and file to unite around the party and implement the new policy, asserting that "we must resolve by all means, at this important stage of our development, the problem of mobilizing the large sum of the capital funds needed for the execution of the First Five Year Plan. This must be done only with our own precious labor." [23]

The policy of self-reliance, like the Maoist concept of mass line, resulted in the development of two important techniques of mobilization and organization. In the process of implementing the new policy line, the Chollima movement was adopted as the "general line" of North Korean development in September 1958, and the Chongsan-ni method was developed as the technique of mass line approach in 1960. The Chollima movement was modeled on the "general line" and the "Great Leap Forward" of Communist China, which began in May 1958 and performed the same function of mobilizing the manpower and natural resources to fulfill the first five-year plan. The Chongsan-ni method, like the hsia-fang (to go to the lower levels) in Communist China in 1957, reshaped the leadership techniques by making closer contact between the cadres and the masses. Thus, the parallel development in China and North Korea was quite apparent.

Almost a decade later, in the 1966-69 period, the North Korean leadership once again engaged in theoretical disputes and policy conflicts over the strategy of economic development when they faced the problems of adjusting to the changing international environment as well as to the changed domestic situation. The rational developmental strategy of the 1961-65 period, which gave priority to the development of light and consumer industry, shifted in 1966 to a policy of further expansion of heavy industry and a defense buildup, even at the expense of light industry and agriculture. Why did such a sudden and drastic shift occur?

One plausible explanation might be that it was a result of the theoretical controversy and policy conflict within the leadership structure. Unlike the policy disputes of the 1956-58 period, the policy-making process in the 1966-69 period was greatly polarized between the two conflicting perspectives of economic development. Faced with such changes in the external environment as the military takeover of South Korea in May 1961, the Cuban missile crisis of October 1962 (in which the Soviet leadership capitulated to the United States), the Sino-Indian border conflict in the fall of 1962 (when Khrushchev supported India), and the escalation of the Vietnam War as well as the normalization of South Korean-Japanese relations in 1964, the North Korean leadership began to reassess their policy position in 1965. From the various policy perspectives presented in the pages of the party newspaper, Nodong Sinmun, and other theoretical journals, we can infer that the policy lines were polarized between the hard line, which pushed for expansion of heavy industry and a defense buildup, and the moderate line, which seemed to insist on the continuation of rational economic development to complete successfully the seven-year economic plan (1961-67). The adoption of a hard-line policy position in the 1966-68 period was the result of the victory of the hard-line faction over the moderate group in the leadership structure.

The conflict between the hard-line policy group and the moderate policy group centered around the question of whether to give priority to the development of defense forces or to continue the rational strategy of proportionate development of heavy industry and light and consumer industry. In these debates the North Korean leaders took seriously into account such external factors as the escalation of the Sino-Soviet conflict, the Cuban missile crisis, and also the growing competition between the rival communist giants, the Soviet Union and Communist China. All of these factors influenced the direction of policy change and the course of economic development in North Korea.

In the course of formulating a new strategy of economic development the moderate group argued for the adoption of a policy of continuing on the "peaceful road to socialism," while the hard-line group pushed hard for a policy giving priority to the development of heavy industry, especially machine-building industry, to supply the defense buildup. The leaders of the moderate group were the two leading Politburo members, Pak Kin-ch'ol (organization director of the KWP's Central Committee and a longtime associate of Kim Il-sung) and Yi Hyo-sun (director of the KWP's Liaison Bureau for Strategy Toward South Korea). They were supported by Kim To-man, a member of the Secretariat in the KWP's Central Committee in charge of the Propaganda and Agitation Department, and Pak Yong-ku, a candidate for membership in the Politburo and a member of the Secretariat. Both Pak Kum-ch'ol and Yi Hyo-sun had been close associates of Kim Il-sung and were elected as regular members of the Politburo of the KWP as well as to the vice chairmanship of the Central Committee of the KWP after the Third Congress in April 1956. It was reported at that time that Pak and Yi ardently supported Kim Il-sung's economic development policy not only during the policy controversy of 1956 but in subsequent years. Kim To-man was even promoted to the Secretariat of the KWP in October 1966, when the party's administrative structure was reorganized.

The hard-line group was apparently led by such military leaders as Kim Ch'ang-pong (minister of defense) and Kim Kwang-hyop (former defense minister and a vice premier); both were members of the Politburo. They were supported by Ch'oe Kwang (chief of the General Staff of the North Korean People's Army) and Ho Pong-hak (director of the General Political Department in the North Korean People's Army), both of whom were candidates for membership in the Politburo. All of them were also five-star generals in active service who wanted to implement the modernization and professionalization of the North Korean army with the support and assistance of the Soviet Union. They also advocated shifting North Korea's policy orientation from Communist China to the Soviet Union in order to solicit more economic aid and technical assistance. They therefore argued for the establishment of a close alliance with the Soviet Union, rather than supporting the Chinese position in the Sino-Soviet conflict, and urged the construction of defensive fortifications throughout North Korea. The rationale for their argument was that China would not really be capable of supplying modern military hardware, as shown in its policy toward North Vietnam, which was then under assault by U.S. military forces, when and if a military attack were directed against North Korea by the military regime in South Korea in collaboration with the U.S. Army.

The intensity of the policy conflict and the severity of the power struggle between these two groups in the 1966-69 period is reflected in the subsequent purges and shift in the policy lines. After the Conference of the Party Representatives in October 1966, the North Korean leadership adopted a hard-line policy of defense fortification throughout North Korea and implemented programs of training more military cadres, recruiting more militia men, and arming and equipping the entire people of North Korea at the expense of continuous economic development. The completion date of the seven-year economic plan was, thus, postponed to 1970. The leaders of the moderate group like Pak Kum-ch'ol (Politburo member and vice chairman of the SPA's

Standing Committee), Yi Hyo-sun (director of strategy toward South Korea), Pak Yong-ku (director of international relations),Yim Ch'un-ch'u (deputy director of policy toward Japan), Kim To-man (director of propoganda and agitation), and Ho Sok-son (director of culture and arts) were all purged from their positions of leadership and policy-making in 1967. Also included in this purge were such governmental leaders as Ko Hyok (vice premier in charge of arts and science), Procurate General Yi Song-un, and Director of North Korea's Central News Agency Pae Chun-ki. [24] Premier Kim Il-sung, as coordinator and manager of the policy-making process, seems to have taken a neutral and independent posture from the beginning of the policy disputes, as he had in the policy disputes of the 1956-58 period.

However, the North Korean leader was gradually convinced of the validity of the hard-line group's proposition in view of the fall of Nikita Khrushchev and the escalation of the war in Vietnam, and he adopted something of a compromise policy line involving further expansion of the defense forces and an independent approach to North Korea's economic development. Reviewing the achievements of the seven-year economic plan, Kim Il-sung asserted that "this has been a period of grim ordeal in which very complex and difficult circumstances were created in our revolution and construction. . . . Frankly speaking, our spending on national defense has been too heavy a burden for us in the light of the small size of the country and its population. Had even a part of the nation's defense spending been diverted to economic construction, our national economy would have developed more rapidly and the living standard of our people improved much more."[25] North Korea needed economic and technical assistance from the Soviet Union to fulfill the plan target, but Soviet aid to North Korea was reduced to a meager 2.6 percent of the state revenue in 1960 and was terminated by 1963, when North Korea aided with Communist China in the Sino-Soviet conflict. The outcome of a series of policy disputes during the 1966-69 period was, thus, a compromise position—an independent and self-reliant policy line that was proclaimed after the Party Conference in October 1966.

The domestic development of North Korea during the 1967-69 period was, in many respects, similar to that of the 1957-59 period because the North Korean leadership reverted to the hard-line policy of relying on the militant and radical appeal of ideology to solve developmental problems rather than relying on material incentives to induce the people to work harder and produce more. Under the hard-line policy, military expenditure jumped to 21.3 percent of the total budget during fiscal year 1967-68 as compared with only 3-8 percent in the years before 1967. [26] The adoption of the hard-line policy was reflected in the militant posture toward the United States and the Republic of Korea. However, the hard-line policy did not last very long: The North Korean leadership once again adopted a moderate policy line in early 1969.

The hard-line group was severely criticized at the Fourth Party Conference of the North Korean People's Army in January 1969 for taking policy positions that were too ambitious and militant and was subsequently purged from the leadership. According to Premier Kim's criticism, the hard-line group pressed hard in the 1965-68 period for an alliance with the Soviet Union that might supply the military equipment for the modernization of the North Korean army. Therefore, they opposed Premier Kim's defense policy of preparing for conventional warfare by recruiting and maintaining the worker-militia at the level of one and one-half million. Furthermore, they failed to obtain military and economic aid from the Soviet Union to carry out the modernization program of the North Korean Army. They were therefore relieved of their leadership positions and were replaced by Ch'oe Hyon (one-time minister of defense and Politburo member), O Chin-u (chief of the General Staff of the North Korean Army), and Kim Yong-chu (organization director of the KWP and Politburo member), all of whom might have been characterized as the moderate group, since the new strategy under their leadership gave priority to the development of light and consumer industry as well as agriculture.

The subsequent course of development seems to indicate that this moderate group was pressing hard to have its policy position accepted by Premier Kim, thus creating a new posture toward the outside world as well as toward domestic development—a little more balanced and rationally calculated. An example of this policy is the North Korean government's announcement of the reduction of its defense expenditure from 31.3 percent of the total budget in 1968 to a meager 17 percent in 1972. The policy dispute over the economic development program was not resolved with the purge of the hard-line group in 1969, however. It still continued at the time the seven-year economic plan was being formulated in 1969-70. A full discussion of this period is presented in the next chapter.

NOTES

1. Nodong Sinmun (The Workers Daily), September 12, 1961.
2. Kim Il-sung, "Central Committee Report to the Fourth Congress of the Korean Workers Party," in ibid.
3. Pravda, February 3, 1955, quoted in Zbigniew K. Brzezinski, The Soviet Bloc: Unity and Conflict, rev. ed. (New York: Praeger Publishers, 1961), p. 156.
4. For analysis of the Sixth Plenum, see Hokusen no Kaiho Chunen: Gin Nitsei Tokusai Seiken no Jittai (North Korea's Ten Years of Liberation: The Reality of the Kim Il-sung Dictatorship) (Tokyo: Nikkan Rodo Tsushin Sha, 1956), p. 122.

5. This work contains accounts of the various communist groups in Siberia, Manchuria, China, and Korea prior to 1925, and has been translated into Russian, Chinese, and Japanese.

6. This and subsequent information on intraparty struggles has been drawn from articles and reports appearing in North Korean publications, as well as in some intelligence reports made by the South Korean government and army. Also in Kim Ch'ang-sun, Pukhan Sip-o-nyon sa (A Fifteen Year History of North Korea) (Seoul: Chimun-Kak, 1961).

7. Nodong Sinmun, December 13, 1960.

8. Nodong Sinmun, October 28, 1963.

9. For the report on the trip, see Nodong Sinmun, August 3, 1956. During this tour the North Korean delegation signed a series of agreements with East Germany, Rumania, Hungary, Czechoslovakia, Bulgaria, Albania, and Poland for economic and cultural cooperation. However, Rumania was perhaps the only country in Eastern Europe that promised to grant a substantial amount of money: 25 million rubles. Mongolia was reported to have promised 5,000 tons of wheat, 50,000 head of sheep, and 20,000 head of cattle.

10. See the editorial "Let Us Protect the Socialist Camp!," Nodong Sinmun, October 28, 1963. This editorial, like the "Origin and Development of Differences between the Leadership of the CPSU and Ourselves—Comment on the Open Letter of the Central Committee of the CPSU" (Editorial Departments of Jenmin Jihpao and Hung Ch'i, 1963), criticized the Soviet policy toward North Korea. This is an important source of information about the Soviet-North Korean conflict.

11. Michel Oksenberg has written an interesting paper on the development of Mao's policy of self-reliance (Tzu-li Keng-sheng). See his unpublished paper on "Mao's Foreign Policy of 'Self-Reliance'" (University Seminar on Modern East Asia: China) (Columbia University, March 4, 1970).

12. For an interesting description of the purge that took place in North Korea in 1956, see Kim Ch'ang-sun, op.cit., pp. 150-162.

13. For its overall development in the Soviet Union and in Eastern Europe, see Brezinski, op.cit.

14. Kim Il-sung, "On Exterminating Dogmatism and Formalism and Establishing Independence in Ideological Work," in Kim Il-sung Sonjip (Selected Works of Kim Il-sung) (Pyongyang: Korean Workers' Party Press, 1960), IV, 325-354.

15. "For a Correct Understanding of Chuch'e," Nodong Sinmun, July 21, 1956.

16. For an interesting analysis of North Korea's behavior, see Glenn D. Paige, "North Korea and the Emulation of Russian and Chinese Behavior," in A. Doak Barnett, ed., Communist Strategies in Asia (New York: Praeger Publishers, 1963), pp. 228-258.

17. For an alaysis of this, see Chalmers Johnson, "Building a Communist Nation in China," in Robert A. Scalapino, ed., The Communist Revolution in Asia (Englewood Cliffs, N.J.: Prentice-Hall, 1969), pp. 52-81.

18. See Kim Il-sung's speech at the mass rally to welcome the Chinese delegation led by Chou En-lai on February 14, 1958, in Wei-le Chao-hsien ti ho-p'ing t'ung-i (For the Peaceful Reunification of Korea) (Peking: Shih-chieh chih-shih ch'u-pan in she, 1958) pp. 19-26.

19. Kim Il-sung, "On Communist Education and Cultivation," Selected Works, op. cit., 116-146.

20. Ibid., p. 143.

21. For a general discussion of the mass line concept developed in China by Mao, see John W. Lewis, Leadership in Communist China (Ithaca, N.Y.: Cornell University Press, 1966), chap. III. Also see Chalmers Johnson, Chinese Communist Leadership and Mass Response: The Yenan Period and the Socialist Education Campaign Period (University of California Center for Chinese Studies, Reprint Series, no. C-6). For a discussion of the mass line approach developed in North Korea, see B. C. Koh, "Ideology and Polictical Control in North Korea," The Journal of Politics, 32, no. 3 (August 1970): 655-674.

22. "At the Central Committee Meeting of the KWP," Nodong Sinmun, December 15, 1956.

23. "For an Effective Fulfillment of the Economic Plan for 1957," Nodong Sinmun, December 16, 1956.

24. For this information, see "North Korea's Political Power and Policy Lines," Asahi Shimbun, February 28, 1968.

25. See Kim Il-sung's report to the Fifth Party Congress, November 2, 1970. It may be found in the Pyongyang Times, November 3, 1970, p. 8.

26. See Kang In-duk, ed., Sege Konsan-kwon Ch'onggam (General Handbook of World Communist Bloc) (Seoul: Institute for Far Eastern Affairs, 1972), p. 971.

5

STRATEGIES OF
ECONOMIC DEVELOPMENT
IN THE 1960s

The seven-year economic development plan was considerably revised and the date of completion was postponed to 1970, a shift in developmental strategy that occurred in 1966. The decade of the 1960s is now characterized as a period of transition from an "agricultural-industrial society" to a mature "socialist industrial society." North Korea is no longer considered a backward agrarian society, and many Western observers, including Harrison Salisbury of the New York Times, have been impressed by its industrial and economic development.[1] How did the North Korean leadership achieve such rapid development in such a short period, and what kind of developmental strategies did they use in accomplishing it? This chapter is primarily an analysis of North Korea's strategy of development in the 1960s in terms of its mobilization techniques, its administrative reorganization to meet the problems of rapid economic development, and the recurring policy disputes over the course and direction of that development.

CHOLLIMA AS A TECHNIQUE OF MASS MOBILIZATION

One can hardly understand North Korea's development in the 1960s without a full knowledge of the Chollima movement which was launched in 1957 and subsequently paralleled the Great Leap Forward movement in the People's Republic of China. Some of the strategies developed by the North Korean leadership in the 1957-60 period were quite similar to Chinese developmental strategy during the Great Leap Forward. Following successful postwar reconstruction (1953-56), which is claimed to have surpassed the industrial output of the prewar period, North Korea embarked on an ambitious five-year economic development plan (1957-61). The recovery of North Korea's economy and industry during the postwar reconstruction period owed a great deal to the massive economic aid and technical assistance provided by the Soviet Union and other Eastern European countries.[2] Therefore, the North Korean leadership formulated their economic development program on the assumption that the Soviet bloc countries would continue to provide aid and assistance at the same level as during the postwar period. However, the international environment changed considerably as a result of the twentieth CPSU Congress, at which Nikita Khrushchev proclaimed the de-Stalinization policy; this was followed by the Sino-Soviet conflict. In this changed mood of international relations in the socialist bloc countries, Premier Kim Il-sung paid a special visit to Moscow and Eastern Europe to obtain economic and technical aid, but he returned home almost empty-handed. Upon his return to Pyongyang he launched a massive program to mobilize domestic resources to pay for the original five-year economic plan instead of revising it. The goals of this program were, of course, "to carry out socialist construction of industry and socialist collectivization of agriculture"; these goals were criticized by Khrushchev as being too ambitious, as discussed earlier.

At the December 1956 Plenum of the Central Committee of the KWP, the party leadership adopted a resolution calling on the entire population to start the Chollima movement, a campaign designed to mobilize human and material resources for the priority development of heavy industry. "In order to overcome the difficulties which have arisen in the domestic and international spheres and also to reach a revolutionary high tide of socialist construction," the party resolution stressed, the KWP must adopt the Chollima movement as the main thrust of mass mobilization.[3] The primary goal of this movement was to combine the programs of cultural and technological revolution in order to succeed in socialist industrialization. Like the Stakhanovite movement of the 1930s in the Soviet Union, the Chollima movement was launched to mobilize the working force and organize them to increase productivity in both industry and agriculture. The campaign for socialist competition to increase production started in the industrial sector but spread quickly into such occupational areas as commerce, education, public health, science, and culture and the arts. Thus, by 1958 the Chollima movement was transformed into a "general line" parallel to the Great Leap Forward in China.[4]

The Chollima movement was similar to the Great Leap Forward in the sense that it was based on the mass line policy, with moralistic fervor and ideological appeal "to increase the maximum productivity and maintain maximum savings," but it was quite different from the Great Leap Forward because the North Korean leadership carefully avoided the mistake of introducing the Chinese style of commune. Though they carried out a total collectivization of agriculture and amalgamated 16,032 agricultural cooperatives into 3,843 basic production units at the li level, they avoided creating larger communes like those in China, which were formed by amalgamating

80

740,000 agricultural producers' cooperatives (APC) into approximately 24,000 people's communes with an average of 5,000 households each. What the North Korean leadership needed to do to justify the mass line policy of the Chollima movement was to formulate a strategy for socialist construction. Kim Il-sung, thus, began to formulate a theory based on the cultural revolution in the countryside and the technological revolution in industry as the prerequisites for successful construction of socialism in North Korea.[5] By alternating his emphasis on the two revolutions—the cultural revolution in 1958-59 and the technological revolution in 1960-63—Kim was able to combine moral and ideological appeal and material incentives in the course of implementing the mass line policy.

The cultural revolution here was meant to step up ideological indoctrination by initiating a new educational program. The indoctrination was designed to eradicate the remnants of traditional ideas from the thought and consciousness of the working masses. The traditional ideas included certain feudalistic and capitalistic notions derived from the ideas of individualism, liberalism, and conservatism. The cultural revolution was, therefore, designed to increase the political and ideological consciousness of the working people so that they might be transformed into dedicated, selfless, and patriotic members of a socialist society. "At the present stage of socialist construction the fundamental task before us is to realize the cultural revolution in order to advance the technological transformation of the people's economy in terms of socialist productivity, and to consolidate further the material and productive basis of socialism."[6]

What Kim Il-sung attempted to achieve in the 1957-59 period was the ideological transformation of his people; this came before the technological transformation of the workers and the intelligentsia. To pay the bills for the industrialization program, the North Korean leadership demanded that the population in general and the peasant masses in particular make sacrifices for a better future. Instead of providing material incentives or investing in the agrarian sector, Kim Il-sung attempted to arouse the enthusiasm and creativity of the working masses by means of ideological and political stimulation. He expounded the thesis that the cultural revolution should precede the technological revolution: "Unless we realize the cultural revolution," Kim asserted, "we won't be able to carry out successfully the technological revolution in our people's economy.[7]

Within the general framework of the cultural revolution, the North Korean government devoted itself to improving the intellectual and technical level of the workers, strengthening public health and medical welfare, and developing the cultural activities of the working class. To comply with the KWP's call to carry out the cultural revolution, the party's propaganda cadres stepped up their activities in November 1958, immediately following Kim's speech, "On the Education of Communism," to the party's activists. It is important to educate the working masses with the spirit of "socialist patriotism" and "proletarian internationalism," according to Kim's speech, because they need to learn to love their working place, their own village and town, and to cultivate their love for the public and state interest rather than being selfish and indifferent to the government's call for socialist industrialization. The working masses can show their love for the country only by participating in the implementation of the mass line policy of the Chollima movement, which is now being elevated to a developmental strategy.

The technological transformation, on the other hand, was designed in the late 1950s primarily to modernize agricultural productivity by introducing irrigation, electrification, and mechanization programs. By the end of 1956, about 80 percent of the North Korean peasantry had already been collectivized, and in 1958, a total collectivization was carried out at the same time that the people's communes were created in China under the banner of the Great Leap Forward. By providing material incentives for the workteam movement, which was launched in 1959, the North Korean leadership attempted to stimulate the working masses to increase productivity. A workteam was organized in each production unit to encourage socialist competition for increased production. The workteam in the industrial plant usually consisted of 20-25 members; those in educational, cultural, and public health institutions often had 50 members. All members took part in the production competition.

According to one report, the small teams were organized in 1958, with only 11,097 managers and technicians leading about 1,368 teams. But the campaign to organize the workteams spread rapidly, reaching more than 3,242 villages within a year.[8] The Red Letter campaign launched by the KWP in September 1958 called on the workers and peasants to join the workteam campaign and take part in the competition to increase productivity. By March 1959, there were more than 8,620 teams with approximately 178,406 members, and the workteam organizations were able to penetrate into every village. "The work team has now spread throughout the country like the flames of fire," one report asserted.[9] The workteam was organized not only in industrial plants but in all other institutions as well. By December 1963, when the organization had grown to 17,057 teams with a membership of 586,403, the breakdown of its membership was as follows: 213,376 workers and clerical personnel, 232,636 members of agricultural cooperatives, and 140,396 students. Thus, the workteam organization succeeded in recruiting more than one million members by July 1965.[10]

By moving into the working masses, Premier Kim demonstrated how to create a model for the conduct of revolutionary work in industry as well as in the village. Between October 6, 1958, and February 2, 1959, Kim Il-sung was reported to have taken part in the actual operation of steel plants in various parts of the country, an experience that yielded such slogans as "Work, study, and live in the spirit of communism. "[11] The workteam had now become the organizational foundation for the mass line policy of the Chollima movement throughout the country. In February 1960, in order to implement the mass line policy, Kim Il-sung went down personally to a rural and backward village, Chongsan-ni, to demonstrate the work of rural development that later served as a model for other villages. Thus, the Chongsan-ni spirit and method became the means of implementing the mass line policy in North Korea in the 1960s.

After the successful completion of the five-year economic development plan (1957-61) in 1960, a year ahead of schedule, the North Korean regime inevitably faced serious problems of administration and management. In the course of solving such administrative problems as the highly centralized and bureaucratized system in industry and the excessively mobilized population in rural areas, the North Korean leadership introduced to important techniques of administration: the Chongsan-ni method for the solution of organizational problems in the agricultural cooperatives and the Taean system for the solution of management problems in the industrial plants. The Chongsan-ni method was, in many respects, a synthesis of two approaches—ideological indoctrination and material incentive—to stimulate the peasant population to increase productivity. The material incentives consisted of awarding prizes, paid vacations, and honorific titles to the workteams that surpassed production quotas. After three years of experimenting with the ideological appeal to the masses to work harder and produce more, the North Korean leaders came to realize that ideological or moral appeals alone would not bring about the desired goals of mass participation and increased productivity. Therefore, they shifted their strategy from ideological stimulation to material incentives, but certain aspects of the ideological appeal were retained. The Chongsan-ni method, thus, incorporated the so-called "independent accounting system" by which the members of the workteam share and take home the extra portion of their production after meeting the established quota. To be precise, this was the profit-sharing principle: The harder the workteam worked and the more it produced, the greater would be its share of the profits after the established quota for the team had been met.

The Chongsan-ni method, as an organizational technique of the mass line policy, used the material incentive system to achieve such goals as increased production of food grains, better planning for cooperative management, and improved organization of the labor force in the countryside. It also introduced the socialist principle of distribution by which the members of the workteam shared the crops and farm produce according to the amount of labor they contributed. The Chongsan-ni method was devised to raise the productivity of the farm cooperatives while sustaining the mass line policy of Premier Kim: "You should learn from the masses. Without going among the masses, you cannot learn. All of you present here are masters of farming. The chairman should openmindedly learn farm work from the peasants, while passing on to them what he knows. "[12] The same organizational techniques were praised extravagantly in the 1960s as Premier Kim's creative application of the general principles of Marxism-Leninism to the unique conditions of North Korea.

After establishing a model for the organizational method of combining ideological appeal with material incentive in their developmental strategy, the North Korean leadership gradually shifted their emphasis from the cultural to the technological revolution during the first phase (1961-64) of the seven-year economic development plan. "During the seven-year period we must carry out the technological revolution and the cultural revolution throughout the country by establishing a material and technological foundation of socialism in order to raise the material and cultural standard of the people, " Kim said in analyzing the current policy.[13] The developmental goals of the technological revolution, therefore, were to increase the production of machine-building industry for the continued development of heavy industry; to implement the mechanization program of agriculture by supplying more tractors and farm machines; to modernize local manufacture by increasing the food-processing industry; and to train more technical cadres by setting up more correspondence and evening schools so that each worker might acquire at least one technical skill. The technological revolution, however, could not be completely separated from the cultural revolution, since these two revolutions are two wheels of a huge cart—socialist industrialization. A single wheel cannot move the cart without the other wheel; therefore, socialist industrialization was to be achieved by combining the two revolutions. Thus, the strategy in the earlier stage of the seven-year plan was formulated on the basis of a rational and scientific approach to the solution of developmental problems.

ADMINISTRATIVE REORGANIZATION AND DISPUTES OVER DEVELOPMENTAL STRATEGY

Developmental changes brought about by the successful accomplishment of the five-year plan by 1960 seem to have forced the North Korean leadership to reorganize the administrative and management system in both industry and agriculture. To meet and solve the administrative problems caused by the centralization, bureaucratization, and routinization of administrative power, the North Korean government decided to decentralize the administrative structure by increasing the participation of the workers in the decision-making and policy implementation processes. The Chongsan-ni method was, as mentioned earlier, introduced to restructure the administration and management of the agricultural cooperatives, while the Taean system was implemented in the industrial plants to provide for greater participation of the industrial

workers in their management. In the course of carrying out this administrative reorganization, three important themes were stressed: decentralization of administrative power from the central government to
the county (kun) government, which had now become the basic-level
government; establishment of a collective leadership system by setting
up a factory party committee along with the management committee; and
sustained emphasis on forceful implementation of the mass line policy
in the administration and management of the industrial plants and the
agricultural cooperatives.

The decentralization of administrative authority was put into
effect when North Korea carried out the reorganization of county government in 1962 by setting up a new administrative organ known as the
county management committee of the cooperative farms.[14] It also
strengthened and increased locally operated industry to make it as
efficient and productive as centrally operated industry. The management committee of the cooperative farms was designed to create a new
administrative organ at the county level and also to introduce the
management techniques of business enterprise into the administration
of the cooperatives. It was to close the vast gap between industrial
management and agricultural administration by transplanting the operational methods of industry into agriculture. "What then are the operational methods of these enterprises?" Kim Il-sung asked. "To provide
the management committee with absolute authority to supervise such
administrative activities as drawing up plans, organizing the work
force, improving technical skills, securing and supplying raw materials,
and managing fiscal matters, " all of which had been handled in the
past by the central government.[15]

Some of the rationale for setting up the management committee was
to maintain a close linkage between the property of "the entire people"
(meaning public property) and the property of cooperatives, which was
actually meant to extend state control over the cooperatives and yet
give the management committee the authority to make decisions. This
committee was different from the state-operated tractor-hiring stations
in the Soviet Union and Eastern Europe in the sense that it not only
provided technical assistance to individual cooperatives but also had
the administrative leadership to direct and coordinate the productive
activities of the cooperatives. The new management committee now
took over the operation of such state-run agencies as the farm-machine
hiring station and the irrigation management office. It was given a
wide range of administrative authority, since it was charged with
drawing up a comprehensive plan for the entire county, thus making
the decentralization of administrative control more effective at the
county level of government.

Prior to the establishment of this management committee, the
Ministry of Agriculture in the central government acted as the "management bureau" of the agricultural sector, but the supervisory function
of the Ministry of Agriculture was now transferred to the provincial

rural management committee, which supervised and coordinated the work of the county management committee under its jurisdiction. Therefore, the Ministry of Agriculture was converted into the Central Agricultural Commission, whose function was to conduct research on such policy questions as how the state ought to improve its agricultural techniques, how to supply and transport the raw materials and farm machines, and how the state should recruit and train the technical cadres to help with rural development. The central commission devoted itself to research work, while the newly created management committee at the county level took full responsibility for administering the coopera- tives. The main thrust of the reorganization was to create a new form of leadership in the administration and management of agriculture by introducing to the agrarian economy the management techniques of business enterprise based on the idea of specialization.

The introduction of a collective leadership system into industrial management also reflected the concept of decentralization in the industrial sector. During the five-year plan period (1957-61), the management system was based on the principle of "one-man manage- ment"; i. e., the manager of each factory took sole responsibility for making decisions and coordinating the quantity and quality of produc- tivity. The industrial workers had no voice whatsoever in the manage- ment and operation of the industrial plant. The Taean system, however, incorporated the concept of collective leadership by which the ordinary workers participate in the planning and decision-making processes through the medium of the factory's party committee. "In this new system, the factory's party committee, as the supreme administrative organ of the plant, manages and runs the factory with direct participa- tion of the party members, the workers and the technicians," Kim Il- sung stressed. "No single person should take the responsibility of managing the plant but every party member, worker, and technician in the plant should take part in the operation of the factory's party com- mittee which is in turn responsible for the administration and manage- ment of the factory."[16] By giving more managerial power to the factory-level committee, the North Korean leadership also aimed to create a sense of participation among the industrial workers.

The mass line policy, as reflected in the Chongsan-ni method and the Taean system, continued to serve as the main strategy of industrial development even after the reorganization of the administrative and managerial systems. The cadres of the central government were instructed to go down to the province and county levels, listen to the problems of the local administrators, and then discuss with them possible solutions to their problems. The local-level administrators were also asked to go among the masses and explain to them the government's policy line, arousing enthusiasm and positive action on the part of the masses by listening to their needs and desires. There- fore, "the mass line is to go into the masses and organize them to implement the party policy correctly by listening to their opinions and suggestions for the solution of local problems, Premier Kim emphasized. "And then the opinions of the masses should be projected back to the higher echelons so that the policy-makers may take their suggestions into account in the formulation of developmental policies. After the formulation of policy on the basis of suggestions offered by the masses, the new directions and policy should be sent down to the masses for execution."[17]

According to Kim-Il-sung, a true leadership technique meant a sincere, voluntary acceptance of the collective leadership on the part of the masses. Therefore, the mass line as a technique of leadership is not a simple discussion between the administrators and the masses, but requires a willingness on the part of the masses to accept the leadership provided by the administrators. Unless this leadership is accepted by the masses, it is nothing but an empty slogan. Therefore, the genuine technique of leadership must be based solely on the mass line approach: going to the masses, listening to their views, and then arousing their enthusiasm to take part in the policy execution. The mass line technique of leadership was particularly stressed when the decentralization program was implemented in industry and agriculture.

The North Korean strategy of industrial development, while still giving priority to the development of heavy industry, continued to pay considerable attention to the development of light and consumer industry, which made remarkable progress during the 1961-63 period. The annual growth rate for 1961-65 was reported at 14.3 percent, even though the projected annual rate of growth during the seven-year plan period was 18 percent. By investing 15.8 percent of the state's total capital investments in the rural economy to improve the standard of living, the North Korean leadership adopted a rational developmental strategy. But this strategy was suddenly shifted in the 1966-69 period to a further expansion of heavy industry and a defense buildup, even at the expense of light industry and agriculture, as discussed in the preceding chapter.[18]

The controversy over the strategy of economic development was not completely resolved even after the purge of the hard-line group in 1969. A group of developmental economic theorists, under the influence of revisionist ideas, argued in favor of slowing the rate of economic growth after the completion of the seven-year economic plan in 1970. In response to this revisionist tendency in economic theory, Premier Kim retorted once again that North Korea could sustain a rate of growth as high as 14 percent each year by combining the strategy of mobilizing revolutionary zeal and enthusiasm to build up industry with that of planned economic development, giving priority to the development of local small-scale industry. However, Premier Kim continues to emphasize the development of human beings as new members of the socialist society along with economic development. His emphasis on the ideological revolution is based on his belief that ideas can be used to create a new socialist man. He therefore stresses in his answers to questions concerning economic growth the idea that "the ideological and cultural revolution to remold the consciousness of the people and enhance their technical and cultural level"[19] is still an essential part of his strategy of development, even after the successful fulfillment of the seven-year plan in 1970.

Those who were under the influence of revisionist ideas were the developmental theorists like Yi Cong-ok (vice premier and chairman of the State Planning Commission), Kim Kwang-hyop (vice premier and former minister of defense), Sok San (vice premier and minister of social security), and Han Sang-tu (ex-minister of finance), all of whom were relieved of their posts in July 1970, when the North Korean cabinet was restructured. Until that reorganization, the North Korean cabinet consisted of 31 ministries and 6 commissions. Following the reorganization, a system of dual administrative control was instituted: First Vice Premier Kim Il continued, as before, to take the full responsibility of formulating the strategy of development, while the second vice premiership was newly created to formulate foreign policy strategy under the leadership of Pak Song-ch'ol, ex-foreign minister; thus North Korea reverted to the rational and moderate posture in both domestic and foreign affairs that had been characteristic of the early 1960s.

DEVELOPMENTAL STRATEGY UNDER THE SIX-YEAR PLAN

If the actual accomplishments of the seven-year development plan are to serve as a reference for a better understanding of developmental strategy in the 1970s, one must contrast them with the projected production targets of the 1971-76 period. As for the overall achievements of the 1960s, Premier Kim has stressed that the country as a whole was transformed from "an industrial-agricultural state" to "a socialist industrial state," which means that it achieved the goal of socialist industrialization.[20] Following the twin goals of socialist industrialization and defense fortification, North Korea has now established a system of defense capable of coping with any external attack. Moreover, political and ideological unity have been consolidated under the banners of three revolutions: the technological, the cultural, and the ideological. In the rural areas the ideological revolution was "the most important and most difficult task that had to be achieved, ahead of all other work."[21]

In the economic and industrial sector, the value of the gross industrial output increased 11.6 times, the means of production 13.2 times, and the value of consumer goods 9.3 times their 1956 levels. Thus, industrial production was reported to have grown at an annual average rate of 19.1 percent during the whole period of socialist construction from 1957 to 1970. However, this growth rate is somewhat misleading, since the average growth rate in the seven-year economic plan period was reported to have been 12.8 percent each year from 1961 to 1970, against the projected rate of 18 percent.[22] This plan had also projected an increase in the gross value of industrial production of approximately 320 percent over the 1960 level during the 1961-67 period, but the actual growth rate for the 1961-70 period was only 2.8 times.

The industrial output of certain sectors showed during the 1961-70 period that the projected output of electricity was 16-17 billion kwh by 1967, but the actual output was reported to have been only 16.5 billion kwh in 1970. The planned target for the production of coal was 23-25 million tons, but the actual output was reportedly 27 million tons; the target of steel production was 2.2-2.5 million tons, but the reported output was only 2.2 million tons. The production target for chemical fertilizer was 1.5-1.7 million tons, but the output in 1970 was 1.5 million tons; the production of cement was 4.5 million tons against the plan target of 4-4.5 million tons. Table 5.1 shows the industrial output in selected areas in the 1961-70 period in contrast to the planned target under the six-year economic development plan (1971-76).

The primary task of the six-year plan is to "consolidate further the material and technical foundation of socialism and free the working people from arduous labor," according to Kim Il's report. Therefore, the value of gross industrial output between 1971 and 1976 is projected to grow by 120 percent, the production of the means of production by 130 percent, and that of consumer goods by 100 percent. During the plan period the average growth rate of 14 percent annually is to be maintained. The development of heavy industry is emphasized in Kim Il's report, but the investment in the development of agriculture and light industry is to be raised, from 20 percent of the total budget in 1970 to more than 22 percent in the 1971-72 period. Thus, the cooperative farmer's income is to be raised 50 percent during the six-year plan period, and the production of such consumer and luxury items as household refrigerators (126,000 units), washing machines (110,000), and television sets (100,000) is to reach new goals.[23]

If the economic performance of the first and second years of the six-year plan in 1971 and 1972 is to serve as any guide to the future direction and course of development in North Korea, the leadership is still committed to pursuing a rational strategy of development under the triple goals of the technical, cultural, and ideological revolutions. North Korea has already reduced its defense expenditure from 31.3 percent in the 1969-70 period to 17 percent in 1972 in order to increase the investment in agriculture and light industry.[24] Thus, North Korea's target for the output of food grains is 7-7.5 million metric tons by 1976, and the differences between the industrial workers and the agricultural workers are to be eliminated by the end of the six-year plan. Unless there is a drastic change in the international environment of North Korea, the present leadership in Pyongyang is very

TABLE 5.1

Selected Industrial Output and Planned Target

	1961	1967 Target[a]	1976 Target
Electricity (1,000 kwh)	9,700,000	16,000,000-17,000,000 (16,500,000)	28,000-30,000
Coal (1,000 tons)	12,000	23,000-25,000 (27,500)	50,000-53,000
Steel (1,000 tons)	790	2,200-2,500 (2,200)	3,500-3,800
Chemical fertilizer (1,000 tons)	700	1,500-1,700 (1,500)	2,800-3,000
Cement (1,000 tons)	2,400	4,000-4,500 (4,500)	7,500-8,000

[a]Actual output by 1970 in parentheses.

Sources: The 1961 figures and the seven-year economic plan targets are from Kim Il-Sung's report to the Fourth KWP Congress in Kim Il-Sung chojak sonjip (Pyongyang: KWP Press, 1968) 3: 77, 113-16; the figures for the actual output in 1970 and the plan target for the seven-year plan are from Kim Il's report, "The Six Year Economic Development Plan (1971-76)," Nodong Sinmun, November 14, 1970.

much committed to carrying out a rational developmental strategy under the banners of three revolutions.

NOTES

1. A series of reports on North Korea appeared in the NEW YORK Times between May 15 and June 7, 1972. Harrison Salisbury has also presented his comparative perspective of North Korean industrial development to the Columbia University Seminar on Korea, October 26, 1972.

2. North Korea received an equivalent of US $1.37 billion in the form of grant-type assistance, loans, and credits. In 1954, foreign aid constituted 33.4 percent of the state revenue, but by 1957 it had dropped to 12.2 percent, and by 1960 it accounted for a meager 2.6 percent of the state revenues.

3. Chao-hsien shih-hui chu-i chien-she chung ti chien-li-ma tso-yueh pan yun-tung (The Chollima Workteam Movement in the Socialist Construction of Korea) (Peking: Shih-che Chih-shih ch'u-pan she, 1962). This booklet is the Chinese translation of the Korean version, which was published by the Korean Workers' Party Publishing House, 1961. I have used the Chinese version throughout this article. See p. 21.

4. Ha Ang-ch'on, "The Chollima Movement Is the General Line of the Korean Workers' Party in the Socialist Construction," Kyo-no Cho-sen (Korea Today), Japanese version, no. 55 (May 1961).

5. See Kim Il-sung's speech for the commemoration of the 10th anniversary of the Korean People's Democratic Republic, September 8, 1958, in Kim Il-Sung Cho-chak-chip (Collected Work of Kim Il-sung) (Tokyo: Mirai-sha, 1970), I, 297.

6. Ibid., I, 313.

7. Ibid., I, 320.

8. The Chollima Workteam Movement, op. cit., p. 21.

9. Ibid., p. 29.

10. Statistical figures for the growth of the workteam may be found in The Chollima Workteam Movement, op. cit., p. 35.

11. Ibid., p. 21.

12. See Kim Il-sung, For the Correct Management of the Socialist Rural Economy (Pyongyang: Foreign Languages Publishing House, 1969), p. 29.

13. Kim Il-sung, "On the Current Tasks of the Korean Democratic People's Republic," speech delivered October 23, 1962, in Collected Work, op. cit., III, 61-62.

14. Sakura-i Ko, "Kita-Chosen ni okeru Sen-ri-ba un-do" ("The Chollima Movement in North Korea"), Chosen Genkyu Greppo (Monthly Report of Korean Research) (Tokyo: Chosen Genkyu-sho), no. 16 (April 1963).

15. Kim Il-sung, "On the Further Strengthening and Developing of the County Management Committee of the Cooperative Farms," in Collected Work, op. cit., III, 124.

16. Kim Il-sung, "On Further Developing the Taean Work System," speech delivered November 9, 1962, in ibid., III, 108.

17. Kim Il-sung, "On the Improvement of the Leadership Cadres' Attitudes toward the Party, the Class and the People and of the Management Activities of the People's Economy," speech delivered December 19, 1964, in ibid., III, 323.

18. This and subsequent facts contained in this section are drawn from such Korean publications as Yon-ku Non-ch'ong (Research Forum) and Kukje Munje (International Questions), publications of the Far Eastern Research Institute, Seoul.

19. Kim Il-sung, "On Some Theoretical Problems of the Socialist Economy," answers to questions raised by scientific and educational workers on March 1, 1969, in Juche: The Speeches and Writings of Kim Il Sung (New York: Grossman Publishers, 1972), 133.

20. See Kim Il-sung's report to the Fifth Congress of the KWP, Nodong Sinmun (The Workers Daily), November 3, 1970.

21. Kim Il-sung, "Theses on the Socialist Rural Question in Our Country," in Juche, op. cit., 71.

22. For Kim Il's report on the Six Year Economic Development Plan (1971-76), see Nodong Sinmun, November 14, 1970.

23. Ibid.

24. See the report of the finance minister (Kim Kyong-nyon), "The Execution of the Budget of 1971 and the Proposal for the Budget of 1972 of the Korean Democratic People's Republic," April 29, 1972, in Chosen Shiryo (The Korean Affairs Monthly) (Tokyo: Korean Affairs Institute), July 1972, 64-92.

6

NORTH KOREA
BETWEEN MOSCOW
AND PEKING

North Korea's relations with the Soviet Union and the People's Republic of China (PRC) in the late 1950s and 1960s were not only shaped by the changing environment of international politics but also influenced directly by the Sino-Soviet conflict. It was in the 1956-57 period that China finally demonstrated its freedom from the Soviet Union and created conditions under which Soviet power could no longer dominate, making itself and the USSR more independent of each other while remaining members of the same system. Under these conditions, the smaller states, like North Korea and North Vietnam, whose freedom of action seemed limited by the attentions of one great power, turned for protection to the other. By "playing off" one independent power against another, the small states had a much higher chance of remaining independent than when there was only one great power in the international communist system.

The escalation of the Sino-Soviet conflict, from the stage of polemical disputes in the late 1950s to that of open warfare in the 1960s, had an enormous impact not only on the political environment of communist societies but also on international relations throughout the world arena. The attitudes and behavior of the North Korean leaders shed some interesting light on the nature and magnitude of the conflict itself and on the development of foreign policy in a small nation like North Korea that was caught up in it. Therefore, to understand North Korea's posture and attitudes toward the Sino-Soviet conflict it seems necessary to survey its relations with both the Soviet Union and China. The development of triangular relations between Pyongyang, Moscow, and Peking for the period from 1956 to 1973 may be divided into three distinct periods paralleling their domestic development (discussed in the preceding chapters). The period of growing independence and self-reliance extends to the 1956-60 period, while the period of neutrality in the Sino-Soviet conflict and the beginning of maneuvering between Moscow and Peking covers the 1961-65 period, and the period of independence and nonalignment extends from 1966 to 1973. This

chapter will also evaluate the changing characteristics of North Korea's
policies on such questions as the reunification of Korea, the withdrawal
of American troops from South Korea, and the increasing role of Japan
against the background of Sino-American and U.S.-Soviet detente in the
1970s.

The most persistent question in the DPRK's foreign policy statements
for the past quarter-century (1948-73) has been how the divided country
should be reunified, without any interference or intervention of foreign
powers, by the Koreans themselves. The goal of North Korea's policy
has been the reunification of the two Koreas, thus making it the most
effective issue for appealing to the national sentiment of the Korean
people. The North Korean authorities blame the United States for the
continued division and the misery accompanying it. Therefore, North
Korea has constantly insisted on the complete withdrawal of foreign
troops from the Korean peninsula so that both North and South Koreans
can achieve the goal of independent and peaceful reunification.

GROWING INDEPENDENCE AND SELF-RELIANCE (1956-60)

Owing largely to the generous economic and and technical assistance provided by the communist countries, post-Korean War rehabilitation and economic development programs (1953-56) were successfully
completed. The Soviet Union generously extended its aid to rebuild the
war-torn economy by granting 1 billion rubles ($250 million) in Septem-
ber 1953. In November 1953, the People's Republic of China signed
with North Korea a 10-year agreement on economic and cultural cooperation, by which Peking waived all debts (approximately $72 million)
incurred by North Korea during the Korean War and granted 8 trillion
yuan ($325.2 million) to be expended over a 4-year period. On the
basis of what they had already achieved during the 1953-56 period, the
North Korean leaders expected to transform their country into a highly
developed modern society by the end of the first five-year economic
development plan (1957-61).

Following the Soviet policy goal of peaceful coexistence, the North
Korean leadership also endorsed the peaceful reunification of Korea at
the Third Party Congress in 1956. It may have been lip service to the
general peace offensive launched by the Khrushchev leadership, but
North Korea was in accord with the Soviet view that international
disputes should be settled by peaceful means. After three years' battle
experience, the North Korean leaders had come to realize that war is
not the only way to win in the struggle against imperialism. Thus,
after the Korean armistice in 1953 they launched a peaceful competition
with the capitalist system in South Korea. Their aim was to build a
socialist economy in North Korea and show the world the superiority
of socialism over capitalism.

However, the most significant impact on North Korea of the changes in the international environment in the late 1950s was clearly the policy of de-Stalinization enunciated by Nikita Khrushchev at the 20th Congress of CPSU in 1956, which brought about the dramatic events in Poland and Hungary.[1] The 1957 Moscow Conference was the major conference of the 12 ruling parties in the post-Stalin era and was a turning point in the international communist movement. Kim Il-sung, who headed the North Korean delegation to the conference, reported on the substance of the conference to the December Plenum of the KWP's Central Committee in 1957 when he returned home. An editorial in Nodong Sinmun, quoting a part of Kim's statement, emphasized the necessity of an independent posture and the development of a self-reliant policy line.

> The important tasks of our Party and our working masses are to fulfill successfully our revolutionary missions, and to participate more consciously in the struggle to make our country strong and prosperous. This is our patriotic mission, and by doing this we can fulfill our obligations to proletarian internationalism and eventually contribute to the strengthening of the socialist camp.[2]

Thus, Kim had changed his emphasis from the interest of the Soviet Union to the need for domestic development—a sign of his growing independence. Under the Stalinist system, Kim's speech indicated, he was a staunch supporter of the Soviet Union; but his posture had changed since the de-Stalinization policy was implemented in 1956. What took place within the Soviet bloc countries in the 1956-60 period is particularly relevant to our analysis and understanding of North Korea's foreign relations, because Kim Il-sung was beginning to denounce and purge some of his associates who had before advocated the Soviet way or the Chinese way of solving domestic problems, including the problem of Kim's personality cult.

North Korea's relations with the Soviet Union began to show stress and strain after Khrushchev's attack on Stalin's personality cult and his initiation of peaceful coexistence. To Kim, the Soviet attack on Stalin's cult of personality constituted the undermining of his own leadership position on the domestic front, and Khrushchev's policy of peaceful coexistence caused him great difficulty in his effort to unify Korea by demanding the withdrawal of U.S. troops. The leadership crisis of August 1956 was, thus, a direct result of Khrushchev's de-Stalinization policy and the "thaw" in the communist world. Moreover, Kim's policy of giving priority to the development of heavy industry in the five-year economic plan (1957-61) was challenged by the coalition leadership of the pro-Soviet and pro-Chinese groups in the KWP. "The party has constantly waged a vigorous ideological struggle against the infiltration of revisionism and all shades of reactionary bourgeois ideas," Kim said in recalling the severity of the ideological and power struggle between himself and his opponents, "and against factionalism. nepotism, and other anti-Marxist ideological elements with the party." Reaffirming his policy line and posture, Kim asserted:

> In particular, with the impetus of the August 1956 Plenary meeting and the Party Conference in March 1958, the Party cleared itself of anti-Party factional elements and attained a great victory in the battle to defend its unity and cohesiveness. The anti-Party factional elements were the enemies of the revolution who were forced to reveal their true colors, no longer able to remain in hiding within the revolutionary ranks as the social revolution became more intense and the class struggle raged fiercely in our country. They were a gang of capitulators and alien elements who degenerated in the face of the arduousness of the revolution.[3]

The foreign policy objectives of North Korea were defined after the Third Party Congress of April 1956 and were formally adopted by the First Session of the Second Supreme People's Assembly in September 1957. The main points of this new policy were the following:

1. to fight for peace by opposing imperialism, because the American-led imperialist forces are the primary source of war and invasion. There is no other way to struggle for peace but to oppose the aggressive war policy of American imperialism.

2. to promote friendship and cooperation with all socialist states.

3. to establish friendly diplomatic relations with all the countries of different social systems, on the basis of the principle of peaceful coexistence, in Asia, Africa, and Latin America.

4. to support the national liberation struggle of every oppressed nation by opposing all forms of colonialism and national oppression.

5. to understand that revisionism and dogmatism are the main danger in the international communist movement. Therefore, North Korea is to conduct a powerful struggle on two fronts to oppose revisionism and dogmatism and then to strive to strengthen the unity of the socialist camp and the solidarity of the international communist movement.

6. to ensure that the principles of Marxism-Leninism and proletarian internationalism are the basis of mutual relations between the socialist states and among the communist and workers' parties. Therefore, the mutual relations of the fraternal parties must be governed by the principles of complete equality and mutual respect.

However, such lofty goals as these must be changed in accordance with shifts in domestic policy and international conditions. As a result of the leadership crisis in August 1956 and the escalation of ideological conflicts between the Soviet Union and China in the 1957-60 period, North Korea's posture and attitudes toward the two communist allies also changed in the late 1950s, when Kim Il-sung established an independent policy line based on his chuch'e idea.

To establish chuch'e in a country means to have an independent and self-sufficient economy. The socialist countries must build a self-sufficient economy to meet the
domestic requirements of diverse overall economic life by
constructing heavy industry with special emphasis on the
machine-building industry and develop light industry and
agriculture simultaneously. Only when we achieve self-
sufficiency in our economy, can we become politically
independent and able to build an advanced modern state.
After establishing a self-sufficient economy, we can carry
out mutual cooperation and specialization of economy, on
the basis of equality and mutual benefit, with other fraternal
countries.[4]

In the 1957-60 period, when North Korea was pursuing an independent and self-sufficient policy in both domestic and foreign affairs,
the Soviet leadership put pressure on certain members of the KWP
leadership to oppose the policy line. Those tactics prompted Kim Il-
sung to charge that "some of the friendly parties were dubious about
our economic policy." Moreover, "the anti-party factional elements
said it was impossible to give priority to the development of heavy
industry. Their assertion was that instead of reconstructing and developing industry and agriculture, we should use aid from other
countries, that is 1,000 million rubles from the Soviet Union, 8,000,000
million yuan from China and the aid from other socialist countries, to
buy consumer goods such as rice and fabrics, and live on them for a
few years."[5] The point of Kim's argument here was to show how correct his policy was, because he had given priority to the development
of heavy industry, and, thus, the grant type of economic aid from the
Soviet Union and China was drastically reduced during the first five-
year economic plan period and transformed into long-term loans. By
1961, foreign aid was not even mentioned in the formulation of the
state budget.

The revisionist trend that followed the liberalization of the
Stalinist system in the Soviet Union became an acute problem. Kim
Il-sung attacked this new trend when he became aware of its potential
to damage his party.

Though revisionism in our country has not appeared in a
systematic way, those who stood against our Party, carried
away by the so-called "international trend," spread revisionism. Thus, in our country, too, there has appeared
the revisionist trend which disrupts the communist movement, opposes Marxist-Leninist principles, and capitulates
to capitalism.[6]

Thus, when the Sino-Soviet conflict was escalating during the 1956-60 period, China attempted to court the North Korean leadership and win their support against the trend of Soviet revisionism. North Korea, being in the same stage of development, could not afford to liberalize its system in accordance with the revisionist trend; therefore, it was ideologically closer to the Chinese view than the Soviet position. China could provide North Korea with ideological inspiration, but what North Korea needed at that stage of development was advanced technology and sophisticated equipment to develop its economy and maintain its defense forces. Thus, North Korea chose to maintain its neutrality by increasing its role as mediator in the Sino-Soviet conflict rather than becoming a supporter of either side.

It was during the 1957-60 period that North Korea adopted its own policy of self-reliance in the course of executing the first five-year plan, and its developmental strategy was closely parallel to that of Communist China. If we analyze North Korea's developmental strategy, we find that the policies of economic development in North Korea were similar to what the Chinese leadership was attempting to accomplish. The policy of self-reliance and the concept of "politics take command," as well as the mass line approach, were enforced in both China and North Korea. The collectivization drive, the Chollima movement, and the Chongsan-ni method paralleled Chinese procedures developed in the Great Leap Forward. Even as early as his first state visit in February 1958, Premier Chou En-lai lauded the correctness of the policy of giving priority to the development of heavy industry during the period of socialist construction.[7]

"Learn from the Soviet Union," the basic policy line during the post-Korean War development period (1953-56), now gave ground to a policy of self-reliance. This policy shift is, perhaps, a key to our understanding of the linkage between domestic and foreign policies based on Kim's chuch'e idea. By 1956, the North Korean leaders claimed that they had overfulfilled the goals set for postwar economic construction (1953-56), thus laying a firm foundation on which the first five-year plan (1957-61) was to be implemented. From the North Korean viewpoint the economic success of the 1953-56 period was due largely to the generous economic aid and technical assistance provided by the Soviet bloc countries. On the basis of what they had already achieved during the 1953-56 period, the North Korean leaders reportedly planned to transform their country into a highly developed modern society by the end of the first five-year plan period. Contrary to their expectations, however, they faced two important problems: the challenge of the so-called "antiparty factionalists" within the KWP, who were directly linked to external powers, and the new development of the de-Stalinization policy and the "thaw" in the communist bloc after the 20th Congress of the CPSU.

In a joint communique issued on February 19, 1958, Premiers Chou En-lai and Kim Il-sung put forward two important foreign policy goals of the two countries: "to strengthen and further develop friendly relations between the two countries and to strive to strengthen the fraternal unity of all socialist countries."[8] The communique stressed, further, that:

> The people of our two countries have in the past endured a long period of mutual struggle in the repelling of invasion. In these struggles, especially in the struggle to repel the invasion of American imperialism, the fresh blood of our precious sons and daughters has consolidated further the traditional friendship that had existed between us.[9]

Even in joint ventures like the construction of socialism, the communique asserted, the "two countries made a further advance in economic, cultural, scientific, and technical cooperation and provided fraternal assistance to one another." Therefore, the primary goals of Chinese and North Korean foreign policy were "to resolve the reunification problems of Korea and reduce tensions in the Far East" by asking all other foreign countries to withdraw their military forces from Korean soil, just as the Chinese People's Republic had already withdrawn its volunteer army from Korea.[10]

From the Chinese and North Korean point of view, the presence of American troops in Taiwan and South Korea was the greatest obstacle to achieving peaceful reunification of Korea and China as well as maintaining peace in Asia. Therefore, the joint communique of 1958 proposed that the United States withdraw its troops from Korea and let the Korean people handle their own problems of reunification.

The return visit of the North Korean delegation, headed by Kim Il-sung, to the People's Republic of China (PRC) in December 1958 not only reaffirmed the foreign policy positions of the two countries, which had been established earlier, but also brought closer economic ties. The Chinese government granted a loan of $105 million beginning in 1960, in addition to the 8 trillion yuan it had granted North Korea between 1953 and 1958. The new loan was to be used to finance deliveries of equipment and technical assistance for industrial development in North Korea. Despite its own economic difficulties, the PRC continued its assistance to Pyongyang. In a series of agreements signed in Peking in October 13, 1960, it also agreed to make a long-term loan of 470 million rubles to North Korea during the 1961-64 period and to assist in the construction of factories there.[11] Thus, China provided $517 million from 1949 to 1964, which represented about 38 percent of the total foreign aid North Korea received, while the Soviet Union provided $550 million, or about 40 percent of the total during the same period. The intensified interaction between China and North Korea that had begun in 1958 resulted in close alliance and cooperation in the 1960s.

Thus, the foreign policy position of the North Korean leadership, like the strategies of domestic development, began to follow an independent and neutral policy line in the late 1950s, but gradually shifted in the early 1960s to support the Chinese position on a number of issues involved in the Sino-Soviet dispute, especially the problems of how to cope with the "American imperialists" who continue to occupy such territories as Taiwan and South Korea.

The Soviet Union's attack on China's Great Leap Forward and commune programs, as well as its support of India during the Sino-Indian border conflict of September 1959, brought about a further escalation of the Sino-Soviet dispute. In July 1960, the Soviet leadership gave the final blow to China when it decided to withdraw all Soviet technicians working in China and refused to honor its promise to provide the blueprint for developing nuclear technology. Against the background of open polemics between the two communist powers, the Conference of Representatives of the 81 Communist and Workers Parties was convened in Moscow in November-December 1960 to iron out the differences and resolve the ideological disputes. The Conference failed to settle the differences, but issued the Moscow Statement after several weeks of consultation and discussion.[12]

A day before the opening of the 1960 Moscow Conference, Nodong Sinmun published an editorial entitled "For the Victory of Marxism-Leninism." In reviewing some of the changes that had taken place since the 1957 Moscow Conference, the editorial pointed out that the 1957 Conference was a turning point in the international communist movement because the individual parties were now able to pursue an independent policy line while maintaining the unity of the socialist camp and the solidarity of the fraternal parties.[13] Commenting on the 1960 Moscow Conference a year later, Kim Il-sung stressed that it was "an event of historic significance in the development of the international communist movement" and said, further, that the Moscow Statement had served as "a program for joint struggle and a guide to action for the communist and workers' parties."[14]

However, Kim reaffirmed his position of independence and neutrality in the Sino-Soviet conflict when he directed his criticism against both revisionism (represented by the Soviet views), which Kim considered the main danger to the international communist movement, and dogmatism (represented by the Chinese position), which "is also harmful to revolutionary work and can become the main danger at particular stages in the development of individual parties." Therefore, Kim told the North Korean party that "without a relentless struggle against revisionism and dogmatism, neither the individual Communist and Workers' Parties nor the international communist movement as a whole can develop, nor can the unity and solidarity of its ranks be ensured." Thus, Kim called on the KWP: "In the future, our Party will continue to struggle manfully on both fronts against revisionism and dogmatism."[15]

NEUTRALITY AND MANEUVERING (1961-65)

North Korea's posture of strict neutrality in the Sino-Soviet conflict and its efforts to maneuver and mediate the disputes in the 1960s began with the signing of a Treaty of Friendship, Cooperation, and Mutual Assistance with the Soviet Union in the Kremlin on July 6, 1961, and with the People's Republic of China in Peking a week later, on July 11, 1961.[16] What led the North Korean leaders to perceive the threat to their security were political events in South Korea and the changing nature of U. S. policy toward East Asia. The ruling elite of North Korea began to perceive that the Kennedy administration's policy toward East Asia was becoming more aggressive and ferocious, and that the success of a military coup in South Korea was a part of America's aggressive policy toward the Korean peninsula. Therefore, Kim rushed to Moscow and Peking in July 1971 to conclude a military pact by which North Korea sought a guarantee of security in case the United States and South Korea made a joint effort to overthrow the North Korean regime.

A joint Korean-Chinese communique issued at the same time made it clear that both parties would remain "consistently and unswervingly faithful" to the Moscow Declaration of 1957 and the Moscow Statement of 1960, when the two parties had agreed that modern revisionism, represented by the leading group of Yugoslavia, was the main danger to the present international communist movement. Therefore, a resolute struggle must be waged against revisionism. Premiers Chou En-lai and Kim Il-sung also pointed out with great emphasis that "U. S. imperialism, the common enemy of the people of the world, is stepping up its aggressive activities and war preparations."[17]

Upon his return to Pyongyang on July 15, Kim Il-sung spoke at a rally of 300,000 people and reported on his successful diplomatic missions, which had won the support and cooperation of both the Soviet Union and China. However, a careful scrutiny of his speech seems to indicate that the North Korean leader was beginning to show signs of strain in his posture of strict neutrality in the Sino-Soviet conflict. Although he used the same amount of space and the same number of words in praising each nation, Kim's tone indicated his warmth and gratitude for Chinese support during the Korean War, which had far outweighed Soviet assistance.[18] Moreover, North Korea's treaty with the Soviet Union stipulated a ten-year expiration date, while the treaty with China had no expiration date at all and provided support to North Korea as long as it was needed. However, the treaties were said to have been of "a strictly peaceful and defensive nature. Their main purpose is to protect the Korean people against imperialist aggression," Kim reported. Moreover, "these treaties are in full accord with the interest of the Korean people and will make a great contribution to strengthening the unity of the socialist camp and consolidating peace in the Far East and the world."

In his report to the Fourth Congress of the KWP on September 11, 1961, Kim Il-sung reaffirmed his position of strict neutrality and independence in the Sino-Soviet conflict when he recognized the contributions of both the Soviet Union and China to North Korea's economic development. "The Soviet people are the liberators and closest friends of our people," Kim said in praise of the Soviet Union. "The Soviet people extended a warm hand of assistance to us and encouraged our struggle whenever our people were confronted with difficulties and ordeals in the course of the struggle to safeguard our country's freedom and independence and to build a new life." Thus, Kim praised the contribution of the Soviet people but failed to mention the Soviet leadership.

As for China's contribution to North Korea, Kim asserted that "the Chinese people are our comrades-in-arms who have shared joys and sorrows, life and death with us in long revolutionary struggles. The Chinese people shed their own blood to aid us at the time of our people's Fatherland Liberation War against the armed invasion of U.S. imperialists. The militant friendship and solidarity firmly established between the Korean and Chinese peoples through their joint struggle against the common enemy are continually being consolidated."[19] From these two statements one can easily surmise that, though Kim tried to maintain a neutral posture toward the two communist allies, his comments about China's contribution showed more warmth and friendliness than his remarks about the Soviet Union.

North Korea's position of strict neutrality in the Sino-Soviet conflict was beginning to waver after the 22nd Congress of the CPSU in October 1961, when Nikita Khrushchev openly attacked Albania. To this attack the Chinese delegation, headed by Premier Chou En-lai, responded with indignation. The North Korean delegation, headed by Kim Il-sung, remained publicly silent, joining 9 other Asian Communist Parties that did not mention the question of Albania. Forty-eight individual delegates from a total of 79 delegations attending the Congress endorsed Khrushchev's attack on Albania, but Kim Il-sung not only supported the Chinese position by withholding his endorsement of Khrushchev's behavior but also became indignant about the whole affair when he returned home and reported to the Enlarged Plenum of the KWP Central Committee on November 27, 1961:

The Albanian question was also discussed at the XXII Congress of the CPSU. Divergent views on a number of questions have cropped up in recent years between the CPSU and the Albanian Party of Labor, and their mutual relations have become abnormal. Much was said about this question at the recent Congress of the CPSU; however, up to now relations with the Albanian Party of Labor have not improved, and a solution to this question still remains to be found. On the contrary, relations between the CPSU and the Albanian

Party of Labor have become further complicated. Should
this situation continue, it will cause grave damage to the
unity of the socialist camp, to the solidarity of the world
Communist movement and to its general development, and
it will be advantageous only to our enemy. [20]

*same as
Non-aligned
bit in
· 78*

Thus, Kim Il-sung showed sympathy for the Albanian leadership
and repudiated Khrushchev's attack. He clearly defended Albania's
position when he stressed the following points:

All fraternal parties are completely equal and independent.
They must formulate their own independent policy based on
the principle of Marxism-Leninism as well as on specific
conditions in their own countries. All the fraternal parties
must learn from each other's rich experience on the basis of
mutual respect, but the question of whether or not to accept
and follow the other party's experience should be determined
by each party on the basis of its own conditions and needs.[21]

The implication of this statement was that North Korea could not
accept the Soviet policies of attacking the cult of personality, reducing the priority on the development of heavy industry, and pursuing an
East-West detente, since North Korea was at a different stage of
development in which it needed strong leadership to carry out its
industrialization programs and to confront the threat of American military
power at a time of unfinished national revolution. The crux of the
matter was that North Korea simply could not agree with the variety of
issues raised in the Soviet policy, especially the elimination of the
personality cult.

Following the 22nd Congress of the CPSU in October 1961, the
Sino-Soviet dispute over many complex issues continued to escalate.
The two nations openly attacked each other's ideological positions.
Since the study and analysis of ideological issues involved in the
Sino-Soviet conflict have been fully explored by other scholars and
are beyond the scope of this chapter,[22] our discussion here will focus
on North Korea's attitudes toward the Soviet Union and China against
the background of the Sino-Soviet competition over the support of North
Korea. Therefore, North Korea's attitudes towards and maneuvers between the two hostile communist powers should be understood and
analyzed against the background of what was taking place in the international arena surrounding Korea, which shaped the North Korean
leaders' perceptions and attitudes toward the great powers.

While the Soviet Union improved its relations with revisionist
Yugoslavia, its attack on dogmatist Albania was further escalated. The
Soviet policy of maintaining friendly relations with Yugoslavia and of
attacking Albania, the closest ally of China in Eastern Europe, inevitably caused the resentment of the Chinese leadership to flare up and

finally led to open polemics and name-calling between Mao Tse-tung and Nikita Khrushchev. Furthermore, the Soviet decision to side with India in the reopening of the Sino-Indian border war and Khrushchev's decision to let Castro down by capitulating to American military power in the Cuban missile crisis of October 1962 seemed to force the Pyongyang leadership to turn to Peking to safeguard their own security. Thus, the editorials and foreign policy statements of North Korea stepped up their attack on revisionism and Yugoslavia as the main dangers to the unity of the international communist movement.

After the policy shift to support the Chinese position in the Sino-Soviet conflict in 1962, the North Korean leadership began to denounce the Soviet Union and to criticize it for entering into collusion with the United States, interfering in the internal affairs of the fraternal parties, and splitting the socialist camp. As the North Korean leadership perceived it, Soviet capitulation to American military might was nothing but a sign of weakness and an indication that the Soviet leadership could not be depended upon. Thus, the North Korean leaders turned to what they perceived to be strong and reliable leadership in the international communist movement, the Chinese. The speeches of Kim Il-sung, like "The Present Task of the Korean Democratic People's Republic of Korea," and the editorials of the party's newspaper, like "Let Us Raise High the Banner of Marxism-Leninism!," clearly express North Korea's disillusionment with the Soviet Union and criticize the Soviet policy of settling disputes by capitulating to the United States.[23]

Following North Korea's change of attitude toward the Soviet Union in 1962, the interaction between China and North Korea became much more active. The Chinese delegation, led by P'eng Chen, paid an official visit to North Korea from April 23 to May 5, 1962, a visit returned by a North Korean delegation led by Pak Kum-ch'ol, vice premier and vice chairman of the KWP's Central Committee, from June 16 to July 2, 1962. The major themes of these two visits were characterized by two slogans: "Chinese-Korean Friendship is Consolidated by Fresh Blood" and "The Eternal Unity of the Chinese and Korean People!" When a North Korean delegation led by Ch'oe Yong-kon, chairman of the Supreme People's Assembly, paid a state visit to China in June 1963 and Liu Shao-ch'i returned the visit in September 1963, a complete change in North Korea's position was apparent. What emerges from these two important interactions between the leaders of China and North Korea is that the North Korean leadership had not only shifted their position to support the Chinese policy line but had also begun openly to attack Soviet behavior in the Sino-Soviet dispute.

An analysis of the speeches and editorial comments as well as the joint communiques issued after each visit indicates clearly why and how the Chinese and North Korean leaders came to full agreement on a variety of issues involved in the Sino-Soviet conflict. First of all, the traditionally close relations between China and Korea were brought even closer when the Korean emigres in Manchuria, led by

Kim Il-sung and Ch'oe Yong-kon, organized the anti-Japanese guerrilla movement in the 1930s and 1940s and fought the common enemy, "Japanese imperialism," shoulder to shoulder with the Chinese people. According to P'eng Chen,

> During the period of the revolutionary civil war and the anti-Japanese War in China, Comrade Kim Il-sung and many other Korean leaders aided in the Chinese people's revolutionary struggle. Moreover, many of the excellent sons and daughters of the Korean people gave their precious lives for the liberation of the Chinese people. On the other hand, during the great liberation war of the Korean people, the Chinese people, like your brothers, sent their precious sons and daughters to participate in the volunteer army to assist you.[24]

Chinese participation in the Korean War was, thus, explained in terms of an expression of appreciation for what the Koreans had done in the 1930s and 1940s to help the Chinese in fighting the Sino-Japanese War. The close ties of these two countries, therefore, should be everlasting, according to the Chinese view, because their relationship had been established on the basis of the common goal of repelling Japanese "imperialism" in the 1930s and American "imperialism" in the 1950s and after. However, the reason for the Chinese decision to send troops to participate in the Korean War, as Allen S. Whiting has demonstrated in his book China Crosses the Yalu, was a complex one, and the decision was probably influenced much more by national security than by the tradition of friendly nations.

Second, the affinity between Communist China and North Korea was further strengthened, according to the Chinese explanation, by the fact that North Korea's socialist construction was modeled after the Chinese policy of "self-reliance" at a comparable stage of development. In his report on North Korean development, P'eng Chen stressed at the meeting of the NPC's Standing Committee that "the Korean people have already made great strides in socialist construction on the basis of a self-sustaining economy and self-reliance. The Korean people, in the spirit of Chollima (flying horse), have already achieved a glorious transformation of the social reality" in North Korea.[25] What P'eng Chen and Liu Shao-ch'i observed in North Korea in 1962 and 1963, respectively, was precisely what they had expected, since North Korea's policy of economic development, like the Chinese model at the comparable stage of development, was giving priority to the development of heavy industry for the goal of a self-sufficient economy. Thus, the common interests of the ruling elite in both countries seem to have brought them closer in their relations as well as in their full agreement on a variety of important issues in the Sino-Soviet conflict.

Third, an important element in the closer relations between Communist China and North Korea, as the Chinese leaders perceived it, was North Korea's consistent support in the Chinese struggle against "revisionism" in the international communist movement, for which the Chinese leaders expressed their special appreciation. "In order to oppose modern revisionism and protect the purity of Marxism-Leninism, the Korean Workers Party carried out a persistent and ceaseless struggle," Liu Shao-ch'i asserted, "and the Korean Workers Party upheld the revolutionary principles of the Moscow Declaration of 1957 and the Statement of 1960."[26] Furthermore, Liu affirmed that "the Korean Workers Party resolutely opposed the anti-Chinese campaign staged by the modern revisionists in order to maintain the unity and solidarity of the socialist camp as well as the international communist movement."[27] Earlier, in June 1963, the joint communique issued by Liu Shao-ch'i and Ch'oe Yong-Kon during the latter's visit to Communist China asserted that ". . . at the present time the main danger in the international communist movement is revisionism." Thus, the policy shift of the North Korean leadership had become apparent by the middle of 1963.

Perhaps the severest of all the indictments directed at the Soviet Union by the North Korean leadership was an editorial entitled "Let Us Defend the Socialist Camp!"[28] This editorial, like the Chinese editorial on "The Origin and Development of Differences between the Leadership of the CPSU and Ourselves," listed a number of crimes that the Soviet leadership had committed in splitting the socialist camp. The differences between the Soviet and North Korean leadership, according to this editorial, could be traced back to the aftermath of the 20th Congress of the CPSU.

According to this editorial, the Soviets had pressured North Korea to accept de-Stalinization and the elimination of the cult of personality, a policy that was actually meant to depose Kim Il-sung. This was the beginning of Soviet interference in the internal affairs of the fraternal party, and the Soviet leaders "had even tried to overthrow the leadership of the fraternal party in the name of the personality cult campaign," the editorial charged. The most revealing fact was the Soviets' attempt to impose their will on North Korean policy both domestically and externally. The Soviet leadership was, thus, charged with having interfered in the policy formulation of building socialism in North Korea, though the Soviet leaders were said to know nothing about North Korean realities. Because the Soviet leadership persistently interfered in the internal affairs of the North Korean party, the editorial charged, "there no longer existed the spirit of equality and mutual respect" in Soviet relations with the North Korean party.

The close relationship between Communist China and North Korea, however, began to cool in 1965, and subsequent events finally led the North Korean leadership to declare a policy of "independence" in October 1966. There were a number of factors that led up to this policy of "independence" in the Sino-Soviet dispute. However, the most important factors were probably the fall of Khrushchev in October 1964 and the further escalation of the Vietnam War. Soviet Premier Kosygin visited North Korea in February 1965. Following this visit, the Soviet Union promised its economic and military aid to Korea, though the figure was not disclosed, and cultural and technical exchange between the two countries became more frequent. By 1968, North Korea's trade with the Soviet Union was 68 percent of the total, while its trade with Communist China was only 11 percent. Another factor that might have led the North Korean leadership to turn away from the Chinese camp was China's unwillingness to undertake the "united action," proposed by Japanese Communist Party Leader Miyamoto Kenji, to counter the escalation of U.S. military action in Vietnam.

A difference of opinion concerning a strategy for coping with the American bombing of North Vietnam seems to have developed between the Chinese party and the North Korean party at just about the same time that the difference of opinion developed between the Japanese party and the Chinese party. The escalation of U.S. military action and the beginning of the bombing of North Vietnam seem to have inten-sified the difference of views between the Chinese and North Korean leadership over the future strategy and tactics that these two countries were to follow in their anti-American and anti-imperialism struggles. Though the North Korean leadership accepted Miyamoto's proposal that they develop a "united front" strategy, the Chinese leadership continued to insist on the settlement of ideological differences before reaching agreement on the strategy of the anti-American struggle. When the Peking leadership condemned the "united front" strategy as a Soviet trick to serve American interests in the Vietnam War, the North Korean and Japanese leadership seem to have turned away from the Chinese camp in the Sino-Soviet dispute. By October 1966, both the North Korean and Japanese parties declared an "independent line" in their relations with the Soviet Union as well as with Communist China.[29]

The Chinese strategy for winning the Vietnam War was the rejection of any cooperation with the Soviet Union until ideological differences were settled. Then the Chinese leadership would cooperate with the Soviet Union in setting up a "second front" in various countries of Asia, including Korea and Japan, organizing independent guerrilla forces, and starting "people's wars" on the basis of what Lin Piao proposed in his now-famous speech, "Long Live the Victory of People's War." However, the North Korean leadership felt that the policy of "united action" would be much more realistic and feasible at the present stage than the settlement of ideological differences because of the American presence in South Korea and the difficulties involved in organizing the guerrilla movement there. In making his own analysis of the Vietnam War and proposing his own strategy to be pursued in Vietnam, Kim Il-sung placed himself in the position of disagreeing with the Chinese. As he put it,

The attitude one takes toward the U.S. imperialist aggression in Vietnam and his attitude toward the Vietnamese people's

struggle should serve as the criterion by which one must
be evaluated, whether a person is actively supporting the
people's liberation struggles or not. A person's views and
attitudes toward the Vietnam question should serve as the
criteria to differentiate two kinds of attitudes: the revolutionary stand and the opportunistic stand; proletarian
internationalism and nationalistic egoism.[30]

The North Korean leadership, therefore, called on all members of the
socialist camp to unite in their efforts to solve the problems of the
Vietnam War. "If the socialist countries unite firmly and bring their
strength into full play," Kim Il-sung asserted, "they can certainly
check any aggressive act of the imperialists."[31] From the North
Korean point of view, "all the socialist countries should, without
exception, pool their strength and come to the aid of the fighting
Vietnamese people, and thus foil the aggression of U. S. imperialism
against Vietnam." However, Kim was very much disappointed because
"the countries of the socialist camp are not keeping step with each
other in opposing U. S. aggression and aiding the Vietnamese people
because of the differences of views among them."[32] Thus, the North
Korean leadership seem to have swung back to the 1966 Soviet position
by accepting the policy of "united action" and rejecting China's
proposal for the settlement of ideological differences before making any
attempt at cooperation.

The uncompromising attitude of the Chinese leadership in the
Sino-Soviet conflict and their unwillingness to formulate a strategy of
"united action" to cope with the American escalation of the Vietnam
War, coupled with the turbulent events of the Great Proletarian Cultural
Revolution in the 1966-68 period, seem to have forced the North Korean
leadership to turn away from Peking.

NONALIGNMENT AND INDEPENDENCE (1966-73)

During the years of the Cultural Revolution in China, neither
cultural nor economic interaction between China and North Korea was
reported, and the Chinese ambassador to North Korea, like all other
ambassadors to foreign countries, was recalled. The stresses and
strains in Chinese-North Korean relations were also reflected in the
Red Guard posters and newspapers during the Cultural Revolution:
They began to attack the North Korean leaders as "fat revisionists and
disciples of Khrushchev." The Chinese leadership was even more out-
raged by North Korean behavior when North Korea sent a delegation
headed by First Vice Premier Kim Il to Moscow in February 1967 to
discuss with the Soviet leaders the "promotion of friendship and cooperation." Perhaps the failure of the Chinese leadership to grant

substantial economic and military aid to fill the void left by the withdrawal of Soviet aid and technical assistance, in addition to the difference over the strategy of "united action" in Vietnam, forced Kim Il-sung to look to Moscow for assistance in 1967. In the 1962-64 period the Chinese supplied $150 million in loans, while the Soviets cut off their aid to North Korea in 1962 after providing some $56 million worth of goods on a long-term basis during the 1961-62 period.

One of the causes of disagreement between China and North Korea during the crucial 1966-68 period was the question of whether or not a communist party like the KWP can still be a correct Marxist-Leninist party while maintaining an "independent" position in the Sino-Soviet conflict. Another issue was whether or not the unity and solidarity of the socialist camp should take precedence over ideological differences among the fraternal parties. On these two questions the North Korean leadership seem to have taken an affirmative position as they called on the other fraternal parties to unite with the Soviets to assist in the Vietnamese struggle. However, the Chinese leadership took a negative attitude and refused to support the Soviet policy of "united action" in Vietnam.

The problems of resisting Chinese pressure were reflected in an editorial in the North Korean party newspaper entitled "Let Us Defend Our Independence!"[33] The editorial asserted that "we should not mechanically imitate the experience of other parties. Therefore, we must conduct our relations with other fraternal parties on the basis of complete equality and mutual respect and oppose both revisionism and dogmatism." The editorial also pointed out that "certain elements of dogmatists and big-power-oriented flunkies who had sneaked into our party vigorously opposed our party's independent policy and criticized out method of adapting other parties' experiences to our conditions. They also pointed out that our party's independent position is nothing but the rejection of our fraternal party's policy line." The editorial also blamed the dogmatists for their insistence that the North Korean party "emulate mechanically the policy position of a certain fraternal party and likewise conduct our foreign and domestic affairs." It is quite obvious that the dogmatists were the pro-Chinese elements in the KWP leadership who pressed hard to support the Chinese policy line in the Sino-Soviet conflict by denouncing the Soviet policy.

By indirectly criticizing China's big-power chauvinism, Kim Il-sung reaffirmed North Korea's policy line of independence and non-alignment at the Second Conference of KWP Representatives in October 1966. In his report to the conference, Kim stressed that the divisive attitudes taken by both the Soviet Union and China were against the principles of Marxism-Leninism and were weakening revolutionary forces around the world. Unity among fraternal parties is urgently needed because disputes bring nothing but aggressive policies of imperialism. Therefore, Kim asserted, it is correct for North Korea to pursue an independent policy line.

When relations between China and North Korea had deteriorated to the point of noninteraction, Soviet-North Korean relations began to improve with the visit of the chairman of the Soviet Council of Ministers, Aleksei N. Kosygin, to Pyongyang in February 1965. Although the Brezhnev-Kosygin leadership resumed economic and military aid to North Korea after the conclusion of a Soviet-North Korean agreement on military assistance in May 1965, the Soviets seem to have failed to meet the expectations of the North Korean leadership. What the Pyongyang leadership desired most was sufficient funds and military assistance so that it might be able to complete its seven-year economic plan (1961-66), which was already behind the planned schedule, and modernize North Korea's weapons and other military equipment. However, the North Korean delegation, led by Ch'oe Yong-kon, took an active part in the 23rd Congress of the CPSU in March 1966, despite the Chinese refusal to attend the Congress, and called for the "united action" of all fraternal parties in the Vietnam War.

In June 1966, a North Korean delegation led by Vice Premier Yi Chu-yon visited Moscow to negotiate an agreement on economic and technical cooperation for the 1967-70 period, by which the Soviets were able to provide substantial loans for North Korea to buy additional machinery and equipment for the completion of the seven-year plan by 1970. Another delegation, led by Defense Minister Kim Ch'ang-pong, flew to Moscow in June 1966 to negotiate with Soviet Defense Minister R. Ia. Malinovski for military aid in order to modernize the North Korean military. However, subsequent events in North Korea and the purge of Defense Minister Kim Ch'ang-pong seem to indicate that he failed to obtain the military aid North Korea needed at that time.

The series of North Korean efforts to obtain advanced military weapons, technological assistance, and economic aid from the Soviet Union, however, must be analyzed in the broad context of what took place in the international environment. In 1965, Japan and South Korea concluded the treaty that normalized their relations after many years of acrimonious negotiations. According to its provisions, Japanese capital and modern technology for economic development were to be brought into South Korea. Furthermore, the United States was continuing to escalate the war in Vietnam by increasing the number of troops and bombing North Vietnam to ashes, while the two communist allies, the Soviet Union and China, were unable to reach an agreement on how to cope with the Vietnam War because of their ideological disputes and conflict of interests. Under those circumstances, the North Korean leadership called on all the fraternal parties to cooperate in united action to assist North Vietnam. However, the Sino-Soviet conflict escalated further, and North Korea's effort to mediate the disputes failed.

Against the background of these developments, First Vice Premier Kim Il paid a prolonged visit to Moscow from February 13 to March 4,

1967, and successfully negotiated an agreement on economic and technical cooperation to help North Korea complete its seven-year economic plan. He agreed to the creation of a Joint Governmental Economic, Scientific, and Technical Council, which was charged with the task of facilitating annual exchange and aid agreements for the 1967-70 period. According to the agreement reached in Moscow in March 1967, the Soviet Union was to provide economic, scientific and technical assistance, more trade, and "cooperation in further strengthening" North Korea's defense potential. An increase in the flow of Soviet aid to North Korea was quite apparent following this agreement, while the relations between China and North Korea continued to deteriorate. Thus, by the early 1970s the Soviet Union could boast that more than 50 industrial projects in North Korea, either under construction or undergoing improvement and expansion, were being assisted by Soviet technicians, funds, and materials.[34]

Following the Ninth Congress of the Chinese Communist Party (CCP) in April 1969, the Chinese leadership seems to have made a serious effort to reevaluate its foreign policy positions, including relations with North Korea, and began to improve its relation with other foreign countries. On October 1, 1969, a North Korean delegation led by Ch'oe Yong-kon attended the 20th anniversary ceremonies of the founding of the PRC, and Ch'oe was placed at the head of the parade among the foreign delegations, indicating that Chinese-North Korean relations were improving. Premier Chou En-lai's visit to North Korea in April 1970 was followed by the appointment of a new Chinese ambassador to Pyongyang, Li Yun-ch'uan. The North Korean ambassador, Hyon Chun-keuk, who had been called home during the Cultural Revolution, returned to his post early in 1970 and was personally received by Premier Chou En-lai. Moreover, in the early spring of 1970 a Chinese trade delegation led by Vice Minister of Foreign Trade Chou Hua-min visited Pyongyang, thus reviving relations between China and North Korea after the conclusion of the Cultural Revolution.

As an indication of the change in China's posture and policy toward the outside world, Chou En-lai paid a state visit to North Korea in April 1970, thus coming full circle in Sino-North Korean relations since his first visit in 1958. Chinese-North Korean relations have now been restored to a normal state in view of what both countries perceive to be a growing threat from a common enemy: American-Japanese collusion in East Asia. The joint communiqué issued in Pyongyang not only denounced the rearmament of Japan but also condemned the American-Japanese plot to convert South Korea into a Japanese military base from which the invasion of North Korea and China will eventually be carried out. However, the Chinese leadership have refrained from support of a North Korean effort to spark revolutionary action in South Korea, and have committed themselves only to defend North Korea from U.S. attack in the future.

111

Furthermore, Chinese Vice Premier Li Hsien-nien ignored the North Korean request for support of its military ventures on the Korean peninsula when the delegation led by Vice Premier Chong Chun-t'aek visited Peking in October 1970. At a banquet on October 15, Chong's speech recalled past military cooperation and expressed confidence in future Chinese support in the event of war. However, Li simply did not make any commitment of military backing to the North Korean government. Instead, Li stressed that the "united strength" of the Chinese and Korean people, with the support of other Asian people, would be sufficient to cope with any "aggressive plots" by the imperialists and reactionaries. To counterbalance North Korean disappointment over the Chinese failure to provide any military support, the Peking government announced on October 17 the simultaneous signing of a 1971-76 trade agreement and economic aid pact.

Thus, in this survey of North Korea's relations with the Soviet Union and China, we can safely conclude that the North Korean leadership shifted its policy position from its close ties with the Soviet Union in the late 1940s and early 1950s to the policy of neutrality and "self-reliance" beginning in 1957 as a result of Soviet refusal to provide necessary economic and technical assistance for North Korean development. This shift was, of course, accelerated by the escalating conflict between China and the Soviet Union over such important issues as the de-Stalinization campaign, the speed and rate of economic development, and the posture and policies of the Soviet Union toward the "imperialist camp" headed by the United States. The Sino-Soviet conflict created a series of leadership crises in the communist world, but the North Korean leadership was able to cope with the domestic repercussions and the challenges of the so-called "anti-party factionalists" within the policy-making circles of the KWP. They have been able to sustain themselves for a long time against any attempt to overthrow them because they can perceive and understand the changing characteristics of the external environment and adjust and adapt themselves quickly to the newly evolving relationships of major powers surrounding the Korean peninsula.

A comparable stage of development in building socialism in China and North Korea seems to have brought the two countries closer in their relations because they share an ideology and an outlook on a variety of important issues in both domestic and foreign policy. The ruling elites of the two nations are determined to transform their backward and agrarian societies into modern industrialized states, utilizing similar methods and techniques of development such as the mass line, self-reliance, and the labor-intensive method in economic development. However, the North Korean leaders have expressed their unwillingness to accept the guidance and direction offered by the Chinese in their relations with other fraternal parties because they feel that a posture of independence and nonalignment is essential to the unity of the international communist movement and the solidarity of fraternal parties. They have also expressed their unwillingness to tolerate great-power chauvinism or intervention in the internal affairs of the fraternal parties. Thus, the North Korean leaders have insisted on maintaining the posture of equality and mutual respect in their relations with China and the Soviet Union manifested in the declaration of independence and nonalignment at the party conference of October 1966. Even in a small nation like North Korea, the leadership has acquired, as a result of the Sino-Soviet conflict, the capacity to maneuver between the two great powers and to engage in diplomacy for its nation's security and best possible interests.

The pattern of power structure in East Asia has been in transition, from the old "bipolar" confrontation to a new accommodation among the four major powers surrounding the Korean peninsula. Following the pronouncement of the Nixon Doctrine and the proposal of the United States to move toward normalization of its relationship with the PRC, a new balance of power among the United States, Japan, the Soviet Union, and China has evolved in East Asia. The situation certainly is a great change from the "bipolar" world of the cold war era to a "multi-polar" world of power balance in the 1970s.

If the emerging new balance among the four major powers leads to the next step of serious negotiations and agreements for the peaceful settlement of conflicts and disputes in East Asia, then the prospects for reunification of Korea will be greatly enhanced. The detentes between the United States and China, on the one hand, and, on the other, the United States and the Soviet Union in the early 1970s have already provided the opportunity for small nations like North and South Korea to reassess their policy positions and explore the possibility of adjusting their posture and policy lines to the changing international environment. One result of the change in the international relations of East Asia has been the agreement between the ruling elites of the two Koreas to come to terms with the question of reunification despite the differences in their ideologies and social systems, as expressed in the North-South Joint Communique of July 4, 1972.[35] Since the goal of Korea's reunification is the single most important aspiration of all Korean people, the leaders in North and South Korea can hardly ignore the issue. No matter how difficult the solution to the problem may be, the ruling elites of Korea are very much committed to resolving the question through peaceful and independent means by 1976, when the two parts of Korea will have completed, according to schedule, their two sets of economic development plans.

NOTES

1. For Khrushchev's attack on Stalin, see The Anti-Stalin Campaign and International Communism: A Selection of Documents, edited

by the Russian Institute, Columbia University (New York: Columbia University Press, 1956).

2. "For the Victory of Marxism-Leninism!," Nodong Sinmun (The Workers Daily), December 7, 1960.

3. Kim Il-sung, "Report on the Work of the Central Committee to the Fourth Congress of the KWP," September 11, 1961, Nodong Sinmun, September 12, 1961.

4. See the editorial in Nodong Sinmun, October 28, 1958.

5. Kim Il-sung, "The Korean People's Army is the Successor to the Anti-Japanese Armed Struggle," speech delivered on February 8, 1958, in Kim Il-sung Sonjip (The Selected Works of Kim Il-sung) (Pyongyang: The Korean Workers Press, 1960), II, 82-83.

6. Kim Il-sung, "For the Successful Fulfillment of the First Five-Year Plan," concluding remarks delivered at the Conference of the KWP on March 6, 1958, in ibid, II, 127.

7. For Chou En-lai's speech, see Wei-le Chao-hsien ti ho-p'ing t'ung-i (For the Peaceful Unification of Korea) (Peking: Shih-Chieh chih-shih ch'u-pan she, 1958), 33-34. This is a collection of speeches by both the Chinese and North Korean leaders as well as editorial comments from Jenmin Jihpao (The People's Daily) and Nodong Sinmun during Chou En-lai's visit to North Korea, February 5-22, 1958.

8. For the Peaceful Unification of Korea, op. cit., 7-12.

9. Ibid.

10. Ibid.

11. Choson Chungang Yongam (The Korean Central Yearbook) (Pyongyang: Korean Central News Agency, 1961), 136.

12. The text of the Moscow Statement is in The Current Digest of the Soviet Press, 12, nos. 48-49 (December 28, 1960, and January 4, 1961). The Moscow Declaration of November 1957 may be found in The New York Times, November 22, 1957.

13. Nodong Sinmun, December 7, 1960.

14. See Kim Il-sung's report to the Fourth Party Congress, Nodong Sinmun, September 12, 1961.

15. Ibid.

16. For the texts of these two treaties, see Pravda, July 7, 1961, and Jenmin Jihpao, July 12, 1961. An English version of the treaties may be found in Documents of Treaties, supp. to Korea Today, no. 63, 1961.

17. For the joint communiqué, see Peking Review, no. 28, July 14, 1961.

18. For Kim Il-sung's speech, see Nodong Sinmun, July 16, 1961.

19. These quotations are from Kim Il-sung's report to the Fourth Party Congress. See Nodong Sinmun, September 12, 1961.

20. This report appeared in Nodong Sinmun, November 28, 1961, and also in the KWP's theoretical journal Kulloja (The Worker), December 1961. The portion with emphasis was omitted by Pravda when it reprinted Kim's speech on December 4, 1961.

21. Ibid.

22. For a general reference work on the Sino-Soviet conflict, see G. F. Hudson et al., The Sino-Soviet Dispute (New York: Praeger Publishers, 1961); Donald Zagoria, The Sino-Soviet Conflict, 1956-1961 (Princeton, N. J.: Princeton University Press, 1962); Alexander Dallin et al., eds., Diversity in International Communism: A Documentary Record, 1961-1963 (New York: Columbia University Press, 1963); William E. Griffith, The Sino-Soviet Relations, 1964-1965 (Cambridge, Mass.: M. I. T. Press, 1967); John Gittings, Survey of the Sino-Soviet Dispute, 1963-1967 (London: Oxford University Press, 1968).

23. Kim Il-sung's speech, "Present Tasks of the Democratic People's Republic of Korea," Nodong Sinmun, October 23, 1962, and the editorial "Let Us Raise Higher the Banner of Marxism-Leninism," Nodong Sinmun, November 17, 1962.

24. For P'eng Chen's speech to the mass rally in Pyongyang, April 24, 1962, see Chung-ch'ao yu-i hsien-hsieh ning-cheng (The Friendship between China and Korea is Hardened by Fresh Blood) (Peking: Jenmin ch'u-pan she, 1962), 3-14.

25. Ibid.

26. Liu Shao-ch'i's speech is in Liu Shao-ch'i chu-hsi fang-wen Chao hsien (Chairman Liu Shao-ch'i's Visit to Korea) (Peking: Jen-min ch'u-pan she, 1963), 5-8.

27. Ibid.

28. "Let Us Defend the Socialist Camp!," editorial in Nodong Sinmun, October 28, 1963.

29. Kyosuke Hirotsu, "Trouble between Comrades: The Japanese Communist Party's Turning Away from Peking," Current Scene, March 15, 1967.

30. Kim Il-sung, "The Present Situation and the Tasks Confronting Our Party," report delivered at the Conference of the KWP, October 5, 1966, Nodong Sinmun, October 6, 1966.

31. Ibid.

32. Ibid.

33. Nodong Sinmun, August 12, 1966.

34. M. Trigubenko, "Twenty Years of Economic and Cultural Cooperation," Mezhdunarodnaya Zhizn, 16, no. 3 (March 1969).

35. For the text of the Joint Communiqué, see The New York Times, July 4, 1972. Also in Choson Ilbo and Dong-A Ilbe, July 4, 1972.

107–08, 109; collected works of,
3; Twenty-Point Program of, 8
Kim Il-sung University, 66
Kim Ilsung-_chui_ ("Kim Ilsungism"),
45
Kim Kwang-hyop, 35, 36, 74, 88
Kim Kyong-nyon, 21
Kim Man-kom, 40
Kim To-man, 36, 54, 74, 75
Kim Tong-kyu, 28, 37
Kim Tu-bong, 6, 67
Kim Yong-chu, 28, 36, 37, 50, 76
Ko Hyok, 54, 75
Korea, 50, 99, 103, 107, 112, 113;
reunification of, 94, 95, 99, 113
Korea, Democratic People's Republic
of (DPRK): Academy of Sciences
of, 1; Central Administration
Council, 39, 40, 41; Central
Agricultural Commission, 86;
Central People's Committee, 39–
41; constitution of (1948), 8, 18,
38, 39; creation of, 7; founder of,
28; Law and Economics Institute,
Academy of Sciences, 2; Ministry
of Agriculture, 85–86; National
Defense Commission, 39; new
constitution (1972), 17–18, 19,
20, 26, 31, 37, 38–40, 41;
president, duties of, 39; State
Administration Council, 39, 40;
ten-point program of, 45 (see
also Korea, North)
Korea, North, 1–22, 26–46, 49–62,
65–76, 79–90, 93–113; Central
News Agency, 75; first five-year
plan (1957–61), 2, 11, 13, 14, 15,
18, 34, 56, 65, 66, 68, 69, 70–71,
72, 79–80, 83, 84, 86, 94, 95, 97,
98; foreign relations, 93–113;
leadership in, 26, 27–46, 49–61,
68, 69, 70, 71–76, 79–88, 89–90,
93, 94, 95–113; People's Army,
74, 76; political culture in, 26,
41–46, 51; seven-year plan (1961–
67), 2, 13, 15, 17, 18, 19, 20, 30,
35, 50, 52, 74, 75, 76, 79, 84, 87,
88–89, 110, 111; six-year plan

(1971–76), 2, 15, 17, 20, 21, 89;
three-year plan, 65; Treaty of
Friendship, Cooperation, and
Mutual Assistance, 101 (see also
Korea, Democratic People's
Republic of (DPRK)
Korea, South, 6, 12, 29, 32, 36, 52,
53–54, 73, 74, 75, 94, 99, 100,
101, 107, 110, 111, 113
Korean Affairs Monthly, 28
Korean Independence League, 6
Korean People's Army, 36, 37
Korean War, 1, 11, 28, 32, 44, 66,
94, 98, 101, 105
Korean Workers Party (KWP), 1, 2,
5, 6–7, 11, 13, 19, 21, 26, 28,
29, 31, 32, 40, 41, 42–43, 53, 54,
55, 56, 59–60, 65, 67, 68, 69, 70,
72, 76, 80, 81, 82, 95, 97, 98,
100, 106, 109, 112: Central Committee, 20, 21, 28, 29, 33, 36,
38, 54, 65, 66, 67, 68, 69, 70,
74, 104 (see also Central Organization Committee [North Korean
Communist Party]); collective
leadership of, 32, 33; democratic
centralism in, 32–33; Fifth Congress, 33, 37, 45, 56; Fifth Congress, documents of, 2; First
Congress, 33; First Party Conference (March 1958), 35, 67,
69, 96, Fourth Congress, 32, 65,
67, 102· Fourth Congress, documents of, 2; growth in membership, 33; Liaison Bureau for
Strategy Toward South Korea, 74·
People's Committee, 5, 7; Plenums
of Central Committee, 13, 21, 36,
54, 66, 67, 70, 72, 80, 95, 96,
102–03; Politburo, 27, 28, 31,
35, 36, 37, 40–41, 54, 66, 74,
76; Propaganda and Agitation
Department, 74; Second Party
Conference (October 1966), 18,
35, 36, 55, 74, 75, 109, 113;
Secretariat, 35, 37, 74; Third
Congress, 35, 65, 66, 69, 74, 94,
96; Third Congress, documents of, 1

ILPYONG J. KIM, Professor of Political Science and Chairman of the East Asian Studies Committee at the University of Connecticut, is an expert on comparative and international politics dealing with the Chinese political system and East Asian affairs.

Before joining the University of Connecticut faculty, Professor Kim taught political science in the Department of Government at Indiana University. He studied comparative communist politics at the Russian Institute of Columbia University in New York and specialized in Sino-Soviet affairs. His theses for the Certificate of the Russian Institute focused on the development of the Korean Communist system in comparison with the Chinese and Soviet political systems, thus laying the foundation from which the present study is drawn.

Professor Kim received his Ph.D. degree from Columbia, writing his dissertation on "Communist Politics in China," later published under the title The Politics of Chinese Communism: Kiangsi Under the Soviets. Dr. Kim is also an author of more than a dozen articles dealing with Communist politics in North Korea and China in such professional journals as The China Quarterly, Pacific Affairs, Journal of Asiatic Affairs, and Problems of Communism.

CHINA AND THE GREAT POWERS: Relations with
the United States, the Soviet Union, and Japan
edited by Francis O. Wilcox

CHINA AND SOUTHEAST ASIA: Peking's Relations
with Revolutionary Movements
Jay Taylor

THE LOGIC OF "MAOISM": Critiques and
Explication
edited by James Chieh Hsiung

THE MODERNIZATION OF A CHINESE SOCIETY:
Taiwan's Path to Development
Yung Wei

THE NEUTRALIZATION OF SOUTHEAST ASIA
Dick Wilson

SOUTHEAST ASIA UNDER THE NEW BALANCE OF POWER *
edited by Sudershan Chawla,
Melvin Gurtov and
Alain-Gerard Marsot

*Also available in paperback as a PSS student edition.

bad:

- intro on comp. communism not
  followed up

- many mistakes of fact

- incredible use of NR
  rhetoric throughout

- empty analysis

good:

- thematic treatment

- focus on factions & leaders of many
  other books avoided, etc